The World Out There

THE
WORLD
OUT
THERE

Becoming Part of the Lesbian and Gay Community

MICHAEL THOMAS FORD

The New Press · New York

© 1996 by Michael Thomas Ford

Library of Congress Cataloging-in-Publication Data

    Ford, Michael Thomas.
      The world out there: becoming part of the lesbian and gay community /
      Michael Thomas Ford.
          p.   cm.
      ISBN 1-56584-333-9 (hc)
      ISBN 1-56584-234-0 (pbk.)
        1. Gay communities—United States. 2. Lesbian communities—United States.
    3. Gay men—United States—Social conditions. 4. Lesbians—United States—Social conditions.
    I. Title.
HQ76.2.U5F671996
    306.76'6—dc20   95-51127
                                                            CIP

Published in the United States by The New Press, New York
Distributed by W. W. Norton & Company, Inc., New York

Established in 1990 as a major alternative to the large, commercial publishing houses,
The New Press is a full-scale nonprofit American book publisher outside
of the university presses. The Press is operated editorially in the public interest,
rather than for private gain; it is committed to publishing in innovative ways works
of educational, cultural, and community value that, despite their intellectual merits,
might not normally be commercially viable. The New Press's editorial offices
are located at the City University of New York.

Book design by Hall Smyth and Gordon Whiteside of BAD

Printed in the United States of America

9 8 7 6 5 4 3 2 1

For my father, who told a little boy that he would be proud of him wherever his life took him, and who has kept his promise.

CONTENTS

The World Out There

ACKNOWLEDGMENTS

This book is about what it means to be part of the lesbian, gay, bisexual, and transgendered community. It is about what I have learned over the past ten years from talking to people, listening to what they have to say, and reading their words. It is because of my extended family, both gay and straight, that this book came about.

For your love, friendship, and inspiration, I thank Katherine Gleason, Mark David Fennell, Linda Smukler, Michael Rowe and Brian McDermid, Anne Corvi and Emma Dryden, Francesca Lia Block, James Garcia, Grace Farrell, June Steffensen Hagen, Tove Jansson, Dorothy Allison, Marilyn Mollenkott, Rev. Paul Zahl, Kate Bornstein, Regina Sackrider and Yasmine Branden, Virginia Agogliati, Nancy Garden, Gregory Maguire, Wickie Stamps, Heather Lewis, Scott Heim, Michael Lowenthal, Pat Califia, Susie Bright, Dorsie Hathaway, Peter McKie, and Andrea Curley.

Most of all, thank you to André Schiffrin and Diane Wachtell of The New Press. Where others saw controversy, you saw a chance to make a difference. And special thanks to Ellen Geiger, who came along just when I needed her and made sure it got done.

AUTHOR'S NOTE

Names are very important. What we call ourselves, or what we are called by others, in many ways defines who and what we are. At the very least, names identify us, either to ourselves or to others, as being part of a particular group, whether that group is a family, an ethnic group, or a social group. Beyond that, names also provide a helpful shorthand with which to recognize one another as having something in common.

This issue of names is very important in the gay and lesbian community, where names take on great significance. For many years the word *gay* has been assumed to include all people who are simply not heterosexual, regardless of color, gender, ethnicity, orientation, predilection, or other unique qualities. The word *lesbian* is also used, of course, but it applies very specifically to women who are emotionally and sexually attracted to other women. Thus, those of us who are not "straight" are expected to be satisfied with being just plain *gay*—a word that doesn't necessarily exclude anyone who isn't a man who is attracted to other men, but really doesn't include them, either. To most people, you are either straight or gay.

Fortunately, we now realize there are many different kinds of people included in the umbrella term *gay community*. Simply not being heterosexual is no longer an adequate or acceptable definition for the many different identities that women and men have. The word *gay* may appear to be a handy catchall for referring to everyone who is not heterosexual, but it really only applies to someone who is exclusively sexually attracted to people of the same sex and essentially only to men attracted to other men. This leaves out whole groups of people, including bisexuals, transgendered people, transsexuals, and those who wish to not adopt any particular label.

So what's the alternative? In recent years the word *queer* has come into vogue with a great number of people, particularly those people who consider using it as taking back a word often used to taunt and hurt us and transforming it into a word of strength. Queer is a good word, and I like it, even though I myself suffered from hearing it thrown at me as a child by those who wanted to demean me. Unlike *gay*, it is an inclusive word that does not carry with it any particular definitions, implied or explicit, about gender, preferences, or anything else. Queer is special, different, not ordinary—all things that gay people are. Because it carries no references to any particular segment of the community, the word queer is entirely inclusive and can be claimed by any of us whose sexuality or mentality is considered different from the norm.

Bisexuals, gay men, lesbians, transgendered people, and transsexuals are all "queer" in the truest sense of the word, even though we might not always have much in common with each other. A transsexual may not necessarily be gay or lesbian, and certainly has different issues than I do as a gay man, but certainly he or she belongs in our larger family because we share similar concerns about equal rights, discrimination, and self-acceptance in a hostile world. It's easy to say we should all just get used to being called *gay*, but the reality is that we aren't all gay. We are all different people with different kinds of lives, and each of us merits to be called whatever we wish to be called, without having to give up a part of our identities for the sake of convenience.

Still, when discussing or writing about bisexuals, gay men, transgendered people, lesbians, and whoever else is out there as a whole group, we need a word that can encompass us all. Otherwise, sentences and books would grow out of control from well-meaning but awkward inclusion.

While *queer* is gaining in popularity of usage, there are still a number of people for whom the word is very painful to hear, dredging up as it does memories of childhood abuse and name-calling. I understand this, and as much as I myself like the word, in writing this book I have decided not to exclusively use *queer* to refer to the larger community. The word *lesbian*, by definition, is specific to women, so I also will not use that word, or the unwieldy phrase *gay and lesbian*, unless it is appropriate. While I am very much aware of the need for the gay community to include women and men equally in discussions about our lives, and of the frequent exclusion of women in these discussions, the phrase *gay and lesbian* is thrown around so much these days, it's starting to sound like a brand name. As well-intentioned as *gay and lesbian* is, in the end it becomes a restrictive phrase in itself.

Thus, I have chosen to use the word *gay* in the text when referring to the community at large. I have done this because, despite its many flaws, it is the word most of us know and recognize to mean women and men whose sexualities are different from those of the mainstream. The word *gay* can, however uncomfortably or inadequately, refer to lesbians, where the reverse is not true. Please understand that unless specifically noted my use of the word *gay* is intended to include gay men, lesbians, bisexuals, transgendered people, transsexuals, and anyone else who feels that she or he belongs in our community. If I am referring only to gay men as a group, I will say so.

While I understand that the word *gay* does not go far enough in including everyone who can be considered part of the gay community, until we have consensus on another word that can even begin to contain the many different kinds of people we are, it is still the easiest shorthand available. At its best, the gay community provides a welcoming home for women and men of many different persuasions and identities. Despite the barriers caused by language, I hope this book does the same, whatever term we use to describe ourselves.

HOW TO USE THIS BOOK

This is a book of information, some of which will be useful to you right now; some of it you might not need or even want until later on. As such, you do not need to read it straight through cover to cover. In fact, I don't recommend doing that. I suggest instead browsing through the sections to see what they entail. Each section deals with a specific topic I think will be of interest to women and men wishing to learn more about the gay community and what role they can play in that community. Some of the sections relate to one another; others stand on their own.

The book also contains a number of profiles of men and women from the gay community. These profiles are meant to give you some idea of the rich diversity of the gay community. Some of these people are well known; others are everyday women and men who could easily live in your community. Each of them is a vital part of the gay community, and each one has something to say about what it means to be a lesbian, gay, bisexual, or transgendered person. None of these people speaks for the gay community; they are simply some of the many different voices that make up our gay family.

There are also a number of sections in the book called "Portraits of a City." These profiles examine how someone wishing to become part of the gay community in a particular city could begin to do that. The profiles are written by women and men who live in those cities and are designed to show the many different ways in which people become involved in their local communities. You do not have to follow the same paths the writers describe; nor are these portraits meant to be complete pictures of any city's gay community. These are simply meant to be examples of how some people used the resources of various cities to start exploring their gay identities. Even if you don't live in these particular cities, you can use many of the same techniques to begin your own journey wherever you are.

Scattered throughout the book you will notice lists of movies, books, artists, schools, and other things that may be of interest to lesbian and gay people. These lists are by no means exhaustive. They are meant to serve as a starting point for those readers who wish to explore things of interest to gay people.

There are no other books on how to become part of the gay community. There are many books about "coming out," about accepting ourselves, and about issues that we might face as gay people; but no one suggests to us how to go about simply being gay. Ten years ago, when I was trying desperately to connect with some kind of gay community, I would have loved to have been able to open a book full of information on how to find other people like myself, on how to start living as a gay man. I hope that this book can provide that kind of information for others.

However, no one book can hope to cover everything there is to know about the ever-fluctuating gay community; this book is only a place to start. Use the ideas you find here to begin reaching out to your own local gay community. Don't worry about whether you're in a huge city or in a small town. We are all in different situations. But we are all also part of a huge family that stretches around the world and is always connected in some way. Finding that family and becoming a part of it is what this book is all about.

BEGINNINGS

As a young gay man growing up in a small farming town in upstate New York, I thought I was the only gay person for miles around. What I knew about gay people came solely from seeing a few gay people on television talk shows and reading about them in a few books, primarily religious ones about sex that my mother kept hidden in the sewing basket upstairs. From these programs and books I discovered that some people thought being gay was a disease or a mental problem, and that all gay people were unhappy and led unfulfilling lives. This didn't sound right to me, but at the same time I didn't know any happy gay people, and I certainly didn't think anyone else at school or in my community could be gay.

I knew that gay people existed, because every June I would see news reports of them marching in parades. Convinced that they all lived in either San Francisco or New York City, I envisioned neighborhoods filled with nothing but gay men and women. For some reason it never occurred to me that all of those happy gay people probably lived somewhere else before they lived in New York or San Francisco, or that a lot of them probably used to live in little towns just like the one I was in. I just assumed that they had always lived in those big cities and that we had nothing in common.

Some of my friends now laugh at my naiveté; others nod knowingly. But the reality is that, despite recognizing myself as gay, I had absolutely no idea what that meant for the rest of my life. I had vague ideas about finding another man and living with him, but I didn't really know what I was going to do with myself or how my life would be different from that of my straight friends. I never really thought about being part of a community of people who were gay like me.

In college, at a small religious school outside of New York where being gay was the worst offense imaginable, I met another gay man, my good friend Jim. We would talk late at night about what being gay meant and about what we would do when we could finally meet other gay people. It sounds funny to me now, but I remember wondering then how I would ever recognize other gay people. I thought there must be some secret that someone wasn't telling me, some special code that gay people used to recognize one another. Jim and I even went to New York City a couple of times looking for other gay people, but we had no idea where to start or what to do, and after walking around for a few hours feeling stupid we just went back home more confused than ever.

When I finally moved into New York to stay, I lived in an apartment in the heart of Greenwich Village, which is a gay neighborhood. I was surrounded by gay stores, gay people, gay bars, gay restaurants, and even gay travel agents and laundries. But despite being right in the center of gay life, I had no idea how to become a part of it. I didn't know how to meet other gay people or how to find gay organizations.

One night, after long deliberation, I went to what I assumed was a gay bar because there were lots of men visible through the windows. I walked around it for what seemed like hours, afraid to go in. Finally, simply because it was freezing and my hands were cold, I went in. There I was in a room filled with other gay men. I was terrified. I'd finally found what I had been looking for, and I didn't know what to do. Eventually someone began to talk to me, and that made it easier. I met a few people that night, some of whom would become friends over the next few months.

Of course that one visit to a bar didn't throw me headlong into New York's gay community. But it made me realize that by reaching out, I could in fact connect with other people like myself. I contacted the city's Lesbian and Gay Community Services Center and became involved with their membership committee. Slowly, I started to meet other women and men with whom I became friends. Over the years, this has led to my involvement in various other groups, from the AIDS activist group ACT-UP to a group of gay writers and editors. Some groups I have been involved with for quite a long time, others for only two or three meetings. Meeting one person leads to meeting another, and even after living in New York for seven years I am still discovering things about the gay community I never knew existed.

Becoming involved with the gay community is an ongoing process. It isn't done by making just one phone call or by going to one meeting. There isn't just one gay organization or one place gay people go to meet other gay people. There isn't a boot camp for gay women and men where we're taught how to be part of a gay team. In some places, the gay community is open and active, with many different organizations and activities available to gay people. In others, the gay community may be almost entirely invisible or may only consist of a few people who get together to talk and have a good time. Most of us find our places in the community by trial and error until we find what we're looking for.

This book is meant to show you some of the many ways in which you can start to become involved with the larger gay community. It is not a book about how to "come out" or to help you decide if you're gay. It is a launching point for you to begin exploring what being gay means for you. For some of the things you will need to be at least somewhat out to do; others you can do no matter what stage of being out you're at. Don't worry about taking the right road or about making a wrong turn. There is no right or wrong way to become involved with such a diverse community. The important thing is that you reach out to others and begin to discover what a rich and wonderful world is out there for gay women and men.

WHAT DOES BEING GAY MEAN?

Before we can begin talking about what being gay means to our lives, it's a good idea to talk a little bit about what being gay is in the first place. We all have many ideas and conceptions about what gay people are and what being gay is. These ideas come from many places, including images on television and in films, from our friends, parents, ministers or rabbis, from sex education classes, books, and from our own imaginations.

Some of these images and concepts are good; a lot of them are most likely bad; and many are just plain confusing. Too often we hear only negative, unpleasant things about gay people. We hear disparaging jokes about "fags" in the locker room. We hear mean things being said about people who other people think are "queers." But what do people mean when they say these things? It is important to understand what being gay is so that we can more easily talk about it.

In the simplest terms, the words *gay* and *lesbian* are used to refer, respectively, to men who are attracted to other men and to women who are attracted to other women. In comparison, people who are attracted to people of the opposite sex are referred to as being "straight." *Bisexuals* are women or men who are attracted to both women and men. We will talk more about bisexuality later in the book, as it is a very important subject and one that is increasingly part of discussions in the gay community. We will also talk further about *transsexuals* and *transgendered people*, people whose physical genders do not match their emotional genders. While these groups are part of the gay community, they have somewhat different issues from those of lesbians and gay men, and these issues are too important to try and explain briefly What's important is that all of these people are part of our gay community.

First, let's examine the words used to define gay men and lesbians. Using *gay* to describe men who are attracted to men probably started as a way to describe men who were flamboyant, as if they were always happy or gay in the sense of being carefree. The word *faggot*, which is also used to describe gay men, does not have quite as pleasant an origin. The term comes from an old word for a bundle of sticks, or faggots. These bundles of wood were used as kindling to get fires burning. In medieval times, gay men were often burned to death by tying them to a stake surrounded by a pile of wood. This was the same method used for killing people suspected of being witches, and in fact many of the men accused of practicing witchcraft are believed to have been gay men being punished for being homosexual.

The word *lesbian* derives from the name given to the people who lived on the Greek island of Lesbos, a thriving center of Greek civilization in the seventh and sixth centuries B.C. One of the island's most celebrated inhabitants was a poet named Sappho. Almost nothing is known about Sappho's life, and only fragments of her beautiful poems survive. But we do know that Sappho taught many young women as students, and that she fell in love with women and wrote about it. Because of this, Lesbos became associated with women who loved women, and the word *lesbian*, which originally simply meant someone who lived on Lesbos, came to mean women who love women.

Other words used to describe lesbians are "dyke" or sometimes "bull dyke" or "bulldagger." The origins of these words is not known exactly, but they became popular in the early 1940s. A "bulldogger" or "bulldagger" was a term used to describe cowboys who wrestled bulls to the ground by grabbing them by the horns. These men were considered very masculine, and since many people thought all lesbians were "mannish," the term may have evolved from those words.

These are all terms that are used for gay and lesbian people. There are many other words, mostly derogatory, that are also used to describe us; but words are just words. So what does being gay or being lesbian really mean?

Most people, including some gay people, think that what makes you gay or lesbian is simply your sexual preference. Yet, this definition does not take into account any other factors about the people or their lives. And while sex is certainly a part of life for many gay people, and is very much part of the definition of who we are as gay men or lesbians, it is only one part of who we are. Some people never have sex, yet they still consider themselves lesbian or gay. Some gay and lesbian people have had sex with people of the opposite sex, but they would never call themselves straight or even bisexual. Many people have had sex with someone of the same sex on one or more occasions but do not consider themselves lesbian or gay. And if you take away a gay person's ability to have sex, she is still gay even though she can't have sex. So there has to be something else that makes us gay.

What is most important in defining what being gay means is not sex but how people feel emotionally. All of us have attractions, to certain colors, to certain tastes, and to certain sounds. Whatever it is we are attracted to, it is something we just feel inside.

When you fall in love with someone, or when you find yourself very attracted to someone, it is usually because of a variety of things. You might like the way she plays baseball, or the way he paints. You might really like his brown eyes or her red hair. It could be something as simple as the way he laughs or the way she smiles at you. Whatever it is, you feel very strongly attracted to a person for many reasons. You feel that being with that person, or with that kind of person, makes you happy and makes you feel alive.

In our society, everything we learn about love, relationships, and sex is focused on straight people. We learn that men fall in love with women and women fall in love with men. We learn that most people get married and have children. No one questions why women find men attractive or why men find women attractive. It's just the way it is, and no one asks why. If you ask a straight woman why she loves men, she probably will say she just likes the way they look, talk, or behave. If you ask a straight man why he likes women, he'll probably say the same things. People don't really know *why* they are attracted to other people; they just know that they are.

Yet lesbians and gay men feel the same things that straight people do, but they feel them for people of the same sex. There isn't

10 NOTABLE LESBIAN AND BISEXUAL WOMEN FROM CURRENT HISTORY

1. **MARTINA NAVRATILOVA:** Tennis player, sportscaster, and mystery writer

2. **AMANDA BEARSE:** Actress and director

3. **URVASHI VAID:** Political leader, activist, lecturer, and writer

4. **MELISSA ETHERIDGE:** Musician

5. **K.D. LANG:** Musician

6. **BILLIE JEAN KING:** Tennis player and newscaster

7. **ROBERTA ACHTENBERG:** Politician

8. **KATE CLINTON:** Comedian and writer

9. **ALICE WALKER:** Writer

10. **ELIZABETH BIRCH:** Activist

anything mysterious about it; it's just what happens. We like being with other people because we relate to the way they think, because they make us feel comfortable, and because we feel they are like us in some deep way. But because we are not taught to view men loving other men or women loving other women as "normal" behavior, it seems out of place. It is seen as something different, and it frightens many people because it doesn't agree with how they've been taught that love works.

But we're not so different from anyone else—we just do things our own way—not "right" or "wrong." Being gay is all about finding people who make us feel comfortable, about feeling like we belong. It's all about falling in love and sharing our lives with other people we care about.

10 NOTABLE GAY AND BISEXUAL MEN FROM CURRENT HISTORY

1. **DAN BUTLER:** Actor and writer

2. **GREG LOUGANIS:** Olympic diver and actor

3. **BARNEY FRANK:** Congressman from Massachusetts

4. **DAVID GEFFEN:** Businessman

5. **ELTON JOHN:** Musician

6. **GERRY STUDDS:** Congressman from Massachusetts

7. **MICHELANGELO SIGNORILE:** Activist, journalist, and writer

8. **LARRY KRAMER:** Activist and writer

9. **SIR IAN MCKELLAN:** Actor

10. **TIM GILL:** Founder of Quark, Inc., a computer software company

There really isn't any *one* definition of what it means to be gay. That meaning stems from each person. It is something you feel deeply, something you just know about yourself because of the ways that you think or feel about yourself and about other people. We are told that being gay means we are many things—most of them bad. We're told we are child molesters, sinners, and perverts. We are told we are demented, sick, and confused. We are seldom told we are happy, healthy, and well-balanced, or that we are kind, loving, and helpful human beings. We are told that something is wrong with us, and that we need help. We are told that we aren't normal.

Gay people are people. We have good points and we have bad points, just like everyone else. But those things have nothing to do with being gay. When it comes right down to it, the definition of a gay person is simply a person with many different qualities, beliefs, thoughts, and feelings who also happens to be emotionally, physically, sexually, and mentally attracted to people of the same sex or to people of both sexes.

It's really that easy. But *being* gay isn't that easy, because it is different from what most of the people around us are. Whether we like it or not, it does make us different, and people are afraid of things that are different. So even though in many ways we are just like everyone else, there are also ways in which we very much are not like everyone else. It's those things that make being gay the wonderful experience it can be, as well as making it the sometimes difficult experience it can be.

WASHINGTON, D.C. — Yasmine Branden

Washington, D.C., is one of the most exciting cities in the country. As the seat of our government, the city is home to many different communities and people from many different ethnic groups. With a host of museums, theaters, historical sites, and concert halls, D.C. offers all of the cultural opportunities of a large city, while just a drive or train ride away from the city there is beautiful country in which to hike, camp, and enjoy the outdoors. The city is also home to a sizable gay community made up of all kinds of people, from women and men involved in national politics to students attending any of D.C.'s several universities.

For anyone unfamiliar with the city, finding the center of gay life in D.C. can be a difficult task. The social atmosphere in D.C. is quieter than in some other cities, and there are no neon signs pointing the way to the gay community. But the subtle signs are everywhere. Scattered among the BMWs, Hondas, and VWs are the telltale rainbow flag bumper stickers, the most obvious of gay insignia. Many apartments are also decorated with the colorful flags or with the equally recognizable pink triangles, indicating that gay people live there.

The highest concentration of gay residents can be found in the hub of gay D.C.: Dupont Circle. "The Circle," as it is known to the initiated, is a neighborhood literally built around a traffic circle. The fountain in the center of the circle is a popular area for gay men and lesbians to gather, sun themselves, walk their dogs, show off their tans, or just casually survey the scene. The Dupont Circle neighborhood fans out in a more or less half circle, loosely bound by Connecticut Avenue, Florida Avenue, and 16th Street NW. Connecticut Avenue, P Street, and 17th Street encompass the majority of gay-owned, gay-friendly, and gay-specific establishments, and are good places to begin exploring the city's gay life. The beacon for people looking for signs of gay life in the circle is easily found under an enormous rainbow flag: Lambda Rising, the largest and oldest gay-owned bookstore in town.

The store provides a wide array of gay and lesbian literature, as well as a convenient meeting place.

Dupont Circle is teeming with gay and lesbian life. On 17th Street you can find eateries offering an endless variety of foods, from Mexican and Cajun fare to steak and Italian. There are also a couple of gay bars. Coffee shops like Pop Stop are also popular places for gay people to hang out with friends. Another popular place to meet other gay people is, of all places, the Safeway supermarket on 17th Street. This may seem odd, but D.C. being the busy place it is, meeting a special friend in the fruit aisle makes perfect sense to the locals!

Lammas Books, at 21st and P Streets NW, is the lesbian counterpart to Lambda Rising, specializing in books, CDs, T-shirts, and other products by and for women. Operated by a knowledgeable, enthusiastic staff, Lammas also sponsors readings by leading women authors. And they have a community affairs center where the interested lesbian can find out what's going on in her community.

P Street also is the nightclub strip. There are at least ten bars for men, although women are welcome and gay men and lesbians often hang out together. The clubs cater to many different types of people, from those who like loud music and dancing to those who just want to sit and relax, from professional people to students and more casual crowds. Again, restaurants abound up and down the street. P Street Beach, a popular meeting place, is just below 24th and P Streets.

Women have slimmer pickings when it comes to meeting places that cater to only female clientele. The oldest women's bar is The Phase, located in Eastern Market on Capitol Hill. The bar is popular with "biker babes," as well as those ascending corporate ladders or working in the halls of government. Many lesbians consider it the most comfortable place to meet and mingle. A hot place for young lesbians is the Hung Jury on Pennsylvania Avenue. Formerly a bar populated by lawyers, it now sports a pool table, dart board, and dance floor. The usual crowd consists of people in their twenties who are casually attired.

D.C.'s gay community likes to celebrate, and there are several times during the year when the community comes out to play. Halloween—or "Hallowqueen" as the locals call it—is the night all of the city's drag queens come out to 17th Street and run down the street in their finest clothes and highest heels. The Annual Drag Race is an institution in the gay community and brings out huge crowds of both gays and straights.

Every year on Father's Day, the gay community throws its biggest and most prominent party—the Freedom Festival. In years past, the Gay Pride Day Parade was a one-day celebration crammed into a small field near P Street Beach. In 1995, a new planning group formed to take over the Pride Day festivities and decided to hold a week-long festival, culminating with a parade that snakes its way from Dupont Circle to Freedom Plaza, one block from the White House. There, the parade participants and crowd find the festival in full swing, with hundreds of booths and a stage for music and speakers.

The nation's capital is perhaps one of the best places for the gay activist to be. Along with San Francisco, Washington has the highest concentration of gay, lesbian, and bisexual political organizations in the country. Gay organizations are a lively component of every D.C. ethnic community as well, and gay groups within these communities are often very active. D.C. is the home of the National Gay & Lesbian Task Force; Human Rights Campaign; the national office of the National Organization for Women; Gertrude Stein; Log Cabin Republicans; many national AIDS agencies; Parents, Friends, and Families of Lesbians and Gays (P-FLAG); and the Gay & Lesbian Victory Fund. Additionally, there are several local gay political groups happy to welcome active gays, lesbians, and bisexuals. The offices of these organizations have information on the gay community in D.C. and are a great place for newcomers to talk to someone from "inside the beltway."

Social groups centered around many different interests and concerns are found in D.C. There are groups that hold meetings for recovering substance abusers, people living with HIV, and personal counseling groups. The Metropolitan Community Church and other gay-friendly churches sponsor support and talk groups, and sports groups are always looking for new faces. D.C. is home to the Lesbian and Gay Chorus of Washington (for which you just have to love to sing) and the Gay Men's Chorus. So, whatever you're into, you're sure to find other people who are too.

For gay young people, the best place to begin learning about Washington's gay community is the Sexual Minority Youth Assistance League (SMYAL). This active organization provides counseling for gay, lesbian, bisexual, transgendered, and questioning young people, and hosts many different social events for gay young people. The various colleges in D.C.—including American University, Georgetown University, Catholic University of America, and George Washington University—all sponsor gay and lesbian student groups, and are also great places to meet other people and find out what is available in D.C. The city is also home to the only university for deaf students, Gallaudet University, which sponsors a group for deaf and hearing impaired gay people.

To find out what's happening in the city, you can always pick up a copy of *The Washington Blade*, D.C.'s weekly free gay newspaper, or *MW*, the metropolitan weekly focusing on entertainment. The *Blade* can be found in almost every shop in Dupont Circle, most bookstores throughout town, and at all suburban Metrorail (the city's subway) stations. In addition to ads for gay and lesbian bars, restaurants, and shops, the papers list upcoming events of interest to gay people.

There are also some drawbacks to life in Washington. For example, the city has a significant crime problem. While anti-gay harassment and attacks are not common, they do sometimes happen, particularly in some of the neighborhoods with little gay presence. While Washington is generally free of some of the conservative attitudes that are prevalent in some southern cities, the politically oriented atmosphere in Washington can sometimes make life feel less relaxed than in other cities. Some people feel that it is harder to meet new people in Washington than it is in some other cities because many people are more concerned about what your job is than who you are as a person. It is common for social groups to form around what people do for work, and some people complain that this makes it hard to make new friends, especially if you are not involved in the political world.

Despite these things, Washington can be a great place to live if you are lesbian or gay. While the politically oriented mood of the city isn't for everyone, D.C. offers many opportunities to become involved in gay life. Because of its size, D.C. offers a wonderful alternative for those people who don't want to live in huge cities but who want to be part of a gay community.

YASMINE BRANDEN lives in a cozy condo between Dupont Circle and Adams Morgan with her partner of three years and their two cats, who suffer from multiple personality disorder. Currently an independent contractor with the National Housing Trust, a nonprofit organization striving to preserve affordable housing, she is the president of the Capital City National Organization for Women, as well as the editor of Capital City Rag. As an activist she has spearheaded protests against the Christian Coalition, Newt Gingrich, GOPAC, and anti-choice and anti-gay/bi groups.

WHAT IS THE GAY COMMUNITY?

Before we talk about some of the ways to start becoming involved with the gay community, it's a good idea to talk about what the gay community is. The answer may seem obvious, but it isn't always that simple.

To many people, the term *gay community* means simply a place where a lot of gay men and women live. But in actuality the gay community is much more than that. The gay community is made up of gay men and lesbians, but it is also made up of people who don't necessarily fit the standard definition of gay people. Besides men who love men and women who love women, the gay community also includes bisexuals, transgendered people, transsexual people, and people who don't use any particular term to identify themselves but whose sexualities set them apart from mainstream straight society. The gay community can at times even include straight people who support gay concerns or who have some connection to gay people.

For many years, people who did not fit the standard definition of being gay did not feel that they were part of the gay community. And often, because of prejudice within the gay community, these people weren't welcome in gay organizations. For example, bisexuals were not necessarily thought about when people talked about the gay community or gay issues. Similarly, transgendered people, or people whose emotional and sexual identities do not match their physical genders, and transsexuals were not represented very well in the gay community. Even something as simple as race or ethnic origins often set some gay people apart from others.

While things are by no means perfect today, the gay community has become much more diverse. We have recognized that, whatever our differences, fundamentally we share a need to have our own community that we can draw on for support. We all need a place where we can feel safe and where we can discuss our concerns, hopes, and fears. We need to be able to talk about our experiences. We need to have organizations that fight for all of our rights as people who are often discriminated against and that make sure our concerns are addressed.

We in the gay community share the common bond of being unique. This does not mean that we need to be apart from everyone else, or that we aren't also very much like people who aren't gay. But the fact is that we are different from other people in many important aspects of our lives, and we need to have a group of people who understand and accept that difference and who share that difference in some way with us. While we may live, work, and socialize with many different kinds of people, we still will always belong to a family of other gay women and men who have had similar experiences.

Our community stretches all over the world. There are gay people in every country and from every culture. We come in every shape, size, and color imaginable. But even though we may not look the same, speak the same language, or have the same beliefs, we are still all part of the same community.

So while it is important to be aware of the global gay community, this book is most concerned with discussing how we find and become part of a local gay community, because that is the community that will affect your life the most. That is the community you will want to become more involved with, the community you will come to know as you explore what being gay and what being part of the gay community can mean in your life.

Yet the gay community takes many different forms. What makes up your particular gay community will depend on where you live and how involved you are in gay life. In a remote area, the gay community may be just a few people who know of one another and who sometimes socialize. In a city like New York, which has a huge gay population, the gay community consists of many thousands of people and hundreds of different organizations.

The gay community also has many facets. Some of these are social: There are gay clubs, bars, bookstores, and restaurants. There are gay dances, gay plays, gay movies, gay parades, and gay sports teams. Other

10

CITIES WITH SIGNIFICANT GAY AND LESBIAN POPULATIONS

1. New York
2. San Francisco
3. Miami
4. Portland, Maine
5. Seattle
6. Houston
7. Washington, D.C.
8. Minneapolis
9. Boston
10. Atlanta

facets of the gay community are political: There are gay politicians, gay rights organizations, and gay activist groups. All of these things together make up the gay community. But each one of these things can also be a community of its own. Your particular "community" may be the people you play with on a gay softball team, or it may be every single person in San Francisco. You can be involved in one area and not in another, or you can be involved in many different areas. We choose our communities by choosing the groups we belong to and the people we associate with. Then, on a wider level, we are also part of the gay community that includes all of us.

In many ways, the gay community is just like any other community centered around people with similar interests or backgrounds. We have concerns, interests, and needs that are specific to gay people. Some things, such as the issue of gays in the military or a presidential candidate's position on gay issues, affect the gay community as a whole. Other things, such as the passage of a city antidiscrimination bill, affect a particular gay community. Some cities have very active gay communities; others have almost no organized gay communities at all. But no matter where we live or how big our local community is, in the end we are all part of the same community, one made up of women and men who, like us, want to live happy, productive lives as gay people.

WHY SHOULD I BECOME INVOLVED IN THE GAY COMMUNITY?

As gay people—especially gay people who may only recently have come to recognize and accept our gay identities—we sometimes feel it would be easier just to stay in the background and be left alone. Getting involved with a gay organization or meeting other gay people seems like a waste of time or too much to ask of us. It may even seem risky or frightening. After all, if you become involved with the gay community, you are saying that you are part of that community. This may not seem like a big deal, but for many people it's very scary suddenly to become part of a group of other gay people.

Relax. Becoming involved with your local gay community doesn't mean that you have to spend every single minute of every single day talking about gay issues or working for gay causes or even talking to other gay people. Becoming involved in your gay community doesn't mean that you suddenly have to tell everyone you've ever known that you're gay or even that you have to march in gay pride parades. It doesn't mean that all of a sudden you're joining some gay army and becoming a totally different person.

What becoming involved in your gay community means is finding out about things that may be of interest or importance to you as a gay person. It means finding out what kinds of things are available to you as a gay person in your community. It might mean reading a gay book or magazine to find out what other gay people are thinking about. It could mean going to a gay club or attending a meeting of a gay group. It might involve visiting a gay community center or volunteering at an AIDS organization.

How you become involved with your community, and to what degree you do it, is up to you. What you do all depends on how comfortable you are with reaching out to others. If for some reason you feel you can't really be "out" as a gay person, you can still be involved with your community just by keeping informed on gay issues or by donating money to gay groups. On the other hand, you might feel ready to jump right in and join a group fighting for gay rights, or you might try writing for a gay newspaper. Or you might just want to join a gay hiking club or a gay students' group and leave the political issues to other people.

Anything you do to find out about the gay community and about what being gay means to you makes both you and the community stronger. You may start by reading about gay issues and move on to attending meetings of a gay group of some kind. That's fine. Later on you might decide that it's time to become more involved. Whatever you do to explore the gay world is another step of enlightenment.

Becoming a part of the community is important for many reasons. On a personal level, becoming involved in your local gay community can help you develop a sense of pride about being gay. Many of us are conditioned to believe that being gay makes us somehow less successful or less important as people. We are taught to hide our gay identities, not to celebrate them. Becoming involved with other gay people allows us to see that there are gay women and men doing wonderful, exciting things and that our community is a vibrant, productive one. It also allows us the freedom to explore our own identities in a positive way.

Reaching out to your local community also means that you will meet new people, many of whom will probably become friends. This may not seem like a big deal, but it is. It's important for us to have other people we can talk to and share with. As gay people, we need to have other gay people around with whom we can be ourselves and enjoy things. We might not always realize it, but living in a "straight" world can be very tiring.

Becoming part of the gay community is also important for a number of larger reasons. For many years, being gay was considered a psychological disorder. Gay women and men were seen as being sick, and sometimes even seen as criminals. Many states had, and some still have, laws forbidding certain sex acts. It was only through the hard work of brave women and men that these things changed for the most part.

Today, it is easy for us to forget that there was a time when being gay could land you in jail. But more and more, gay rights and gay people are coming under attack by an increasingly conservative segment of the population. In some states, like Colorado and Maine, there are very active campaigns to make gay rights laws illegal and also to make it a crime even to discuss gay issues in schools. More and more, gay-themed books are being banned in libraries across the country. Gay people are routinely attacked and even killed by people who see us as being a threat to their sense of morality. Gay parents have their children taken away by the courts, and gay people who want to adopt children are often told that they can't.

It's very painful to read about these things or to see them firsthand. And it's very tempting to remain quiet when they happen and not draw attention to ourselves. As more and more men and women stand up for gay rights, politicians and people in power have had to listen. And the more visible we become, the more our enemies try to keep us down. But by becoming involved in our communities, we are saying that we will not let people take away our rights, harass us, or undo everything for which gay people have worked so hard. The more we stand up for ourselves and demand to be treated with respect, the more people who hate us want to hurt us.

The gay community is at a very interesting and very crucial point in its history. We are demanding that we be treated equally under the law, and we are telling the world that we will not simply be content to sit quietly and pretend we don't really exist. The world in general is no longer able to push gay issues aside. Politicians must address gay issues if they want to be elected, and more and more gay people are themselves being elected to public office. This is a great thing. But we are also now being challenged more often.

In the next few years, some extremely important decisions will be made that concern gay rights and how the gay community lives, decisions about issues such as legal gay marriages, gays in the military, antidiscrimination laws, and laws about everything from whether or not gay issues can be taught in classrooms to whether or not gay people can adopt children. Now, more than ever before, the gay community needs to be educated and to be able to fight for our rights. If we don't, there is a good chance that these rights will be taken away from us.

Unfortunately, the gay community has not always fought successfully. Many people have just assumed that their rights would stay intact. But as we are seeing, this isn't necessarily true. That's why it is extremely important that we all be involved in our community, both on a local and an international scale. Again, this doesn't mean that every one of us has to run for office or campaign for gay rights. What it means is that we have to be educated enough to know what our community is fighting for and what challenges we are facing.

Most of us don't have children, but we should all be concerned about whether or not young people can be taught positively about homosexuality in school. We don't all want to live in Oregon, but we should all be concerned about the fight that the gay community there is waging against right-wing Christian groups who want the community gone. We need to be educated so that we can vote effectively, discuss issues effectively, and simply know what is going on in the world regarding gay people.

Becoming involved in the gay community in whatever capacity provides a little bit more support. Each time you buy a gay book or attend a meeting of a gay group, whether it's a writers' discussion group or a rally for AIDS education or lesbian health issues, you are reinforcing a sense of community. The more we are united as a community, the harder it is for people to beat us down or ignore us.

If you are a young person, don't think that there isn't any way for you to become involved in the gay community. All across the country groups are being created especially to address the needs and concerns of gay young people. Some of these groups are part of local gay community centers; others are separate groups started by people who want to reach out to young people. They can be excellent places for you to begin finding out what is available to you as a gay person in your area, and they can also be great places to meet other people your age.

Young people are especially important to the gay community because they are the next generation of gay people. Many gay people do not come out and start to become involved in the gay community until they become older. Now we are seeing many more people becoming involved in community life when they are in college and even in high school. This is very important for the gay community because it means that we have people who understand gay issues at an earlier age and who are able to integrate gay issues into their lives.

When you become involved in the gay community, no matter what age you are, you are helping yourself by letting yourself enjoy the people and the life of the community, and you are helping the community itself by lending your support and your voice. This not only benefits you, but it benefits the many women and men, especially young people, who might still be struggling with coming out.

MELISSA ETHERIDGE: MUSICIAN

One of the most popular singers today, Melissa Etheridge sings and plays hard-edged rock and roll that has earned her comparisons to Janis Joplin and Bruce Springsteen. When she came out as a lesbian in 1993, she surprised straight fans and delighted gay ones. Her albums *Melissa Etheridge* and *Brave and Crazy* had already made her a favorite with both gay and straight audiences. After coming out, her popularity skyrocketed, proving wrong the long-held belief that gay performers would not be accepted by straight audiences. Her third album, *Yes I Am*, was released several months after her announcement of her sexuality and became a huge seller, staying on the charts for more than two years and earning her a Grammy award for "Best Rock Performance by a Female." She became the first openly gay woman to appear on the cover of *Rolling Stone* magazine, and she performed to sold-out audiences wherever she went. Her fourth album, *Your Little Secret*, also became a monster hit, making her one of the most successful performers in rock music.

Growing up in Leavenworth, Kansas, Melissa felt, as many gay young people do, that she was the only person in the world dealing with what she was feeling inside, even though she didn't know exactly what those feelings meant. "I always thought I was the only one," she says. "I felt very different and alienated, not by other people, but by the feelings that I had. It made me think in my head that I was different, and I didn't understand what it was. Then later, in high school, some kids could be vicious to me, calling me a 'queer' or other names. I didn't quite take it personally for a while because I thought they were just bad words. I didn't actually associate those words with myself until later."

When she did begin to associate those words with herself, she was confused. She responded to her feelings by turning to her music. "When I was in high school I felt a lot of frustration, which I poured into my music," she says. "It wasn't until I left high school that I

found a gay community and started to understand what it all meant." Finding herself in a supportive community, Melissa also started playing her music for other people, and they responded enthusiastically. As her popularity grew outside the gay community, so did questions about her personal life, which she avoided answering. Many gay people recognized something in Melissa and her songs that they connected with, but she remained in the closet on the advice of managers and other people in the record industry.

Then, in 1993, Melissa came out in front of a huge audience at the Triangle Ball, a gay function held as part of the inaugural celebrations for President Bill Clinton, whom Melissa had actively supported in the 1992 campaign. She was there that evening along with her friend k.d. lang, another singer who had come out as a lesbian several months earlier. "k.d. and I talked in-depth before she came out," Melissa says, "and I urged her to do it. Then she did, and it was wonderful, and I was thinking, 'I told her to do it, so why can't I do it myself?' Then she and I were both at the Triangle Ball, and I was filled with so much pride and so much good feeling being with all of those other gay people that I just came out right there on the spot."

Despite some speculation that coming out might hurt her career, Melissa experienced no negative response. "I didn't even get one single record returned to me," she says happily. In fact, the support Melissa has received from both straight and gay fans has been amazing. Most important, she is proud of herself for being open about her life. "I just like the honesty of it all," she explains. "I always hated the 'we're just not going to talk about it' routine when people asked about my personal life. And that's the worst part, because to some extent you're perpetuating a lie. You do things to keep the myth going, and it takes a lot of energy and it's very hard."

When asked about the difficulty people in the public eye face when deciding to come out, Etheridge says, "When you have become successful, sometimes it's easier to come out because you already have that success to stand on. But when you are successful and you come

out, you aren't just coming out to your family or friends. You're coming out to the whole world. And to be judged by the whole world is really unusual and strange."

Now that she has come out, Melissa certainly is out to the whole world. She has became an outspoken supporter of many different issues, including gay rights and AIDS concerns. "The anti-gay forces are so full of hate and fear," she says, referring to one of the issues she feels most strongly about. "It's really awful what they're trying to do to gay people and what they say about us." She also is very concerned with helping gay young people. "I think the more of us that come forward, the easier it will be for young people to accept themselves. It's hard growing up whether you're straight or gay, but gay kids have an even harder time because [they] have nothing that speaks to [them] about [their] experiences. There are no movies about our lives." And she is making a difference. "I don't see most of my audience, because I'm up on stage," she says. "But I get a lot of letters and a lot of people coming backstage telling me that my being out has helped them. That's great to hear."

While Melissa is very actively involved in the gay community, music is still her first love. She believes it is important to reach out to all kinds of people. "I enjoy having my music listened to and made personal by many different types of people—men and women, straight and gay. I think music is good that way."

Melissa's advice to gay people struggling with their feelings is simple. "Believe. Believe in yourself. Believe that the feelings and emotions and urges that you have are genuine and that unfortunately we live in a time when people are just coming around to understanding them. There will be those people who tell you it's wrong, but love is never wrong. You can't say that any good feeling toward somebody else is wrong. And believe that you are not alone. There are millions of us. And believe that you are good, that being gay is a good thing you should be proud of."

FINDING THE GAY COMMUNITY

When I was growing up, I thought I was the only gay person I knew. I thought I was the only gay person in my school, in my town, and even in the largest city nearby. I didn't know of any famous gay people, or even any nonfamous ones. I knew that there were other gay people somewhere, but I thought they all lived in big cities like New York and San Francisco.

Since then I have found out that at least three other boys in my high school class are gay. I also know now that many of the brothers and sisters of people I knew are gay. It turns out that quite a few people in my hometown are gay, and I even found out that two of my relatives are. Gay people are everywhere, even when we don't see each other right away.

The problem most often mentioned by lesbian and gay people, especially young gay people, is that there seems to be no one else around who understands what they are going through. The fact is, most gay people think they're the only ones for miles around who are gay. But the good news is, it isn't true.

The gay community is one both global and local. But it is also often an invisible community. Why? Because lesbian, bisexual, gay, and transgendered people come from so many ethnic groups. We don't all look the same. We don't all act the same. Being gay is not like being Jewish or being Italian—you can't recognize other people in your "family" just by the way they look, the color of their skin, what their names are, or anything else. But no matter what we look like, where we live, or what our jobs and interests are, we all have something in common. We are all gay, and that makes us all part of the same family, despite all of our differences.

There are a lot of studies that say different things about how many people are gay. People who don't want to admit that there are gay people say there aren't very many. Other people say there are dozens around every corner. Whatever people say, it is generally accepted that about 10 percent of the population is gay or lesbian.

So why can't we seem to find these people when we need them? Because many of them aren't out. And the chances are that they look and act just like anyone else. And if you're not out, then they aren't going to know where to find you. You're going to be walking around each other all the time without knowing about each other. For all you know, the woman who sells you your morning coffee at the deli is gay, and so is the guy who fixed your transmission. And both of them might think they're the only ones around too.

So how do you start finding other gay people? If you're in an area with a large population, you can most likely find at least one gay organization nearby. Many cities have lesbian and gay community centers, where various gay groups meet. Even if there isn't an organized center, there may be a local gay group, hotline, or social group. The easiest way to find these places is simply to look in the phone book under *gay.* If you don't find anything there, you might also try calling a local women's group or a group such as Planned Parenthood. Often these types of groups will know of any local lesbian and gay groups. Local AIDS organizations are also great places to start if you're looking for information on gay groups in your area, as many gay groups support AIDS causes.

If you are a young person, you can start looking right in your own school or college. Many colleges, and even some high schools, now have support groups for lesbian, gay, and bisexual students. The most obvious way to find other gay young people is to find a group that has already been created. When I was growing up, there were no groups especially for gay young people to get together and talk about their lives. Now, though, many parts of the country have groups just for lesbian, gay, bisexual, and transgendered youth. Some of these groups are social groups, where gay young people meet and just hang out. Others are support groups led by counselors who work with gay youth. Some of the more well-known groups are run by Boston Area Gay and Lesbian Youth (BAGLY), the Hetrick-Martin Institute in New York City, and the Sexual Minority Youth Assistance League (SMYAL) in Washington, D.C.

You can also look at the resource guide in the back of this book to see if there are groups in your area. New groups are being created all the time, so if you don't see a group listed for your area, do some looking around. The chances are you'll find at least one group in your area that can help you meet new people.

Many small groups are springing up all over the country when young people decide to get together with other gay people. Some of these form in local lesbian and gay community centers; others form in high schools and colleges. If you live near a college or university, you might want to find out if they have any gay groups that meet there. You can do this by calling the school's student activities office and just asking when and where the group meets. While the people who attend the groups may be older than you are, it is a good place to start meeting people in a relaxed setting.

If there are no groups in your area, and you really want to take a big step, you can start your own. You could do this through a gay community center, or you could try to start one in your school or college. If you try to start a gay support group in your school, you will probably encounter some resistance from school authorities. But usually if you can find a teacher who will agree to help sponsor the group, you should have the right to form it even if the school tries to tell you that you can't. Many young gay people have formed talk groups for students at their schools and found that, slowly, more and more people start to come.

Even without the help of a group, you can still probably find gay people right around you. First, look to your friends. It may seem odd to think that you wouldn't know if a friend is gay or not, but he or she may not know that you are either. We tend to attract friends who are like us in many ways, even ways we can't really define. It's possible that some of your friends are drawn to you, and you to them, because you both somehow sense that you're gay. My best friend from college is someone who lived down the hall from me. We became friends because we found out that we both liked to write and liked music. It wasn't until almost a year later that we found out we are both gay. So don't rule out people you never thought of as possibly being gay.

Another way to look for other gay people is to look at people in clubs you might belong to. As stereotypical as it might sound, many gay men do belong to the drama club or the chorus, and many lesbians do play sports. If you are gay and in a club, then maybe someone else in the club, chorus, or team is too. You don't have to go and ask each one; you can hint around in other ways. You can start a conversation about something else, like music or movies or books, that can allow you to ask certain questions without risking too much.

If you have a job, you might also be able to meet other gay people at work. A lot of young people who work in clothing stores, record stores, and other places where young people go, say that they often meet other gay people there. For example, if you watch what kinds of records or books a person looks at or buys, you might get a clue as to whether or not he or she is gay. If a young woman comes up to the counter with a k.d. lang CD, or the book *Annie on My Mind* by Nancy Garden, you could try starting a conversation by telling her what you thought of the album or book. If a guy is looking at Barbra Streisand records, he might be buying one for his girlfriend, but chances are he wouldn't mind having another gay guy to talk to. Just starting a conversation by saying, "Is that a good record?" can lead to making a new friend.

Whether you're a young person or not, another way to find other gay people is to know some gay codes. By "codes" I mean little clues that can tell you if someone is gay or not, or that can let others know you are gay without having to wear a big sign around your neck. For example, most of us know that a pink triangle is a symbol of the gay community. The pink triangle was originally used by Nazi soldiers in World War II to designate prisoners who were lesbian or gay. It was sewn onto their clothes. Sometimes lesbians were made to wear black triangles. Today, the pink and black triangles are symbols of gay pride, and many people wear them in the forms of pins or earrings or on clothing. Other symbols of gay pride include the symbols for Mars and Venus—the Mars sign looks like this: ♂, and the Venus symbol like this: ♀. These symbols, especially if you see two of the same that are interlocked are often worn by gay men and lesbians. If you see people wearing any of these symbols, chances are they're gay, and you might want to talk to them. And if you wear them, other people may recognize them as well and talk to you.

Another gay sign is the rainbow flag. The rainbow flag is simply a flag made up of different colored stripes. The different colors are meant to represent the many different types of people in our community. Many gay people hang rainbow flags in front of their houses or put rainbow flag stickers on their cars to show gay pride and to let other gay people know that they aren't alone. This can be especially useful in areas where gay people are not very visible. You may also want to look for stores or businesses that have rainbow flags hanging outside them or have rainbow flag stickers on their windows. Chances are that the people who own them are gay, and you might meet some more gay people if you go inside.

If you live in an area that has no gay community centers or groups for gay people (and many people do), there are still ways for you to connect with the gay community. One increasingly popular way is through computers. As more and more people become familiar with computers and what they can do, many groups form around different needs and interests. This includes lesbian and gay groups. Most online services such as Prodigy, America Online, Compu-Serve, Delphi, and eWorld feature hundreds and even thousands of different meeting places for people with similar interests. All of them have folders where gay people can leave messages and talk about things that interest and concern them. Many of these areas have special folders just for gay young people as well.

How do you find these areas? If you are already connected to one of these programs, you can find the gay areas by using the search or key word command and typing in the word *gay*. This should automatically take you to the correct area. Then it's just a matter of searching around for a while until you find what you're looking for. America Online, the service that I use, has several areas specifically for gay people. There is even a folder under the Gay Message Boards section of the Gay and Lesbian Community Forum that is especially for gay and lesbian teens. Many young people leave messages there to connect with other people, to talk about problems

GETTING ONLINE

There are many different online services available today. Four of the most popular ones are listed here. Each of these services has a gay and lesbian forum. You may also want to look in your city for other online services, which are frequently cheaper and allow more extensive access to the Internet and the World Wide Web.

To order the software necessary to connect with these online services, simply call the numbers given or write for free software. Make sure that you indicate whether you have a Macintosh system or a PC system.

AMERICA ONLINE

1-800-301-9966 ⬅
8619 Westwood Center Drive
Vienna, VA 22182-2220

America Online has a gay and lesbian community forum featuring chat rooms, folders for virtually every interest, and a resource file of gay and lesbian organizations. Also featured is Lambda Rising bookstore's online area, where subscribers can order books, read reviews, and chat with authors.

COMPUSERVE

1-800-881-8961 ←
5000 Arlington Centre
Boulevard
PO Box 20961
Columbus, OH 43220-9910

PRODIGY

1-800-PRODIGY ←
PO Box 8667
Gray, TN 37615-9967

Similar to America Online, CompuServe and Prodigy feature various areas of interest to gay and lesbian people, including chat rooms and folders for various interest groups.

EWORLD ←

The online service of choice for many Macintosh users, eWorld features a gay and lesbian "village" called QWorld. You can obtain free software by calling 1-800-521-1515, ext. 969. Merchants and professionals who want to list their products or services can send e-mail to beckqw@eworld.com or write to QWorld, PO Box 49088, Atlanta, GA 30359.

they're having, or just to chat.

Online services are becoming more and more complex, and there are many different uses for them. Some gay online services feature extensive lists of national and local organizations. Others feature news of interest to the gay community. For people who are not near an active gay community, these services can keep them up to date on gay issues as well as provide a means of contacting other gay people around the country. Even people who are involved in their communities can benefit from online services by making contact with gay people around the world, discussing issues with other people, and simply making new friends.

If you aren't already connected to an online service, then you need to buy the software that allows your computer to dial up through a modem to connect to the service. This software is available for free by calling the company you are interested in using, and it also often appears attached to computer magazines. You can also buy software for connecting to various online services at most software stores.

Another good way to stay connected to the gay community is through magazines. There are several excellent magazines specifically for gay, lesbian, bisexual, and transgendered people, all of which are available at newsstands or by subscription. The oldest and best-known gay magazine is *The Advocate*, a biweekly news-magazine featuring news articles about gay issues around the world, interviews with people of interest to the gay community, as well as entertainment news and book, record, and film reviews.

There are several magazines specifically for gay men, including *Genre* and *Men's Style*, which feature articles about health, fitness, entertainment, sports, and other topics of interest to men, while magazines such as *Curve* and *Girlfriends* cater to lesbians. *Out* is for both women and men. *Tapestry* is a magazine for transgendered people. Addresses for all of these publications can be found in the resource guide at the back of this book.

Obviously, those of us who live in areas with large gay populations have more opportunities for meeting other gay people. But no matter where you live, there are probably other gay people. You might just have to look harder to find them. And even if you can't find any other gay people, you can always be connected to the gay community through computers, magazines, and other avenues. The important thing to know is that these things are available to you.

ATLANTA, GEORGIA — Margaret Maree

First-time visitors and natives alike marvel at Atlanta's sprawling green space, its top-flight convention arena, stellar array of international restaurants guaranteed to satisfy even the most fickle palate, and friendly yet diverse population that rivals just about any fast-paced American city these days. Looking for Tara? Expecting to find dimwitted bubbas in pickup trucks? Think these homegrowns are clueless and just waiting for someone to show them how to get off the farm? Think again. Though not New York or San Francisco, this is the New South.

Atlanta continues to snare more than its share of attention, due as much to the Olympic Games and world-class hometown braggarts like Ted Turner and Newt Gingrich as to its image as a Southern gay mecca. In a city of 3.5 million, surrounded by seventeen metropolitan counties, there is a range of voices here that is impressive. None more so than among the estimated 300,000 gays and lesbians who call Atlanta home. Reflected in the mix are African Americans and Asian Pacific Islanders, Zen Buddhists and Baptists, kayakers and two-stepping cowboys, Harvard alumnae, lesbian moms, a raging leather/S-M community, a boatload of golf-playing good old boys (and girls), a plethora of AIDS-related organizations, and an emerging support network for gay and lesbian youth.

Ironically, with all the newcomers the gay and lesbian community in Atlanta can seem hard to find, when in fact gays permeate every facet of life—every profession and every neighborhood. The upside of this is obvious, but it can be overwhelming for someone new to town trying to navigate through to the gay culture. And with a bevy of colleges and universities centered downtown, most gay-friendly neighborhoods—Virginia-Highland, Little Five Points, Inman Park, and Emory/Decatur—have as much a student look as a queer social scene.

It's crucial to remember that, precisely because Atlanta covers so much geography and has neighborhoods that seem to blend into each other, there really is no one place to find the gay community. But the quickest way to start is through the network of gay businesses in midtown, the overwhelmingly gay neighborhood: bookstores, restaurants, museums, and coffee shops all appropriately located in the epicenter of the city. Nearly all gay and lesbian endeavors radiate from midtown, which is mostly gay male and marked by gentrified, Victorian-inflected brownstones that overlook the rolling hills of Piedmont Park. The park is the site of the annual gay pride festival and seasonal city-sponsored jazz, theater performances, and cultural festivals. Many new gay businesses, theaters, visual arts groups, and clubs—like the new downtown jazz and piano bar that's packed every weekend with a diverse mix of women and men—are constantly opening in or near downtown.

The easiest way to find out what's happening in gay Atlanta is to pick up one of the weekly gay publications, *Southern Voice* or *Etc...* at Outwrite Books or Brushstrokes near Ansley Park. Both have a complete list of up-to-the-minute calendar listings, social and organizational. It's also a good idea to grab a copy of the monthly *Venus Magazine*, which gives an overview of the substantial gay African-American community and a range of all local intown activities and gallery showings.

While Atlanta does not have one active central community center, there are two organizations that provide similar functions. The Atlanta Gay Center (63 12th Street; 404-876-5372) offers some services, including a program for lesbian and gay young adults. More active is the Lambda Center, comprised of some of the city's most active gay and lesbian political organizers. As of this writing, the Lambda center is in search of a permanent address, so it is advisable to look for the center in the phone book or call information for a current telephone number.

Lesbian and gay youth fare well in Atlanta. There are many colleges in the area, including Emory University, Georgia State University, Georgia Institute of Technology, Spelman College, Agnes Scott

College, Oglethorpe University, and Kennesaw College, and each has a student group for lesbian, gay, and bisexual students.

In addition, Atlanta is home to an exciting number of programs for young adults. YouthPride (404-815-9965) provides counseling and support solely for people aged 13 to 24. The Atlanta Gay Center (404-876-5372) offers resources to gays and lesbians and bisexuals aged 14 to 24. Meetings are Thursdays 6:30-8:00 P.M., free of charge, and address self-esteem, coming out, safe sex, and teen AIDS. The center also coordinates youth recreational activities and offers an on-site health clinic Monday through Thursday 5:30-9:00 P.M. The Georgia Association of Pastoral Care (404-636-1457) is a network of thirteen theologically based but nondenominational counseling centers with support groups and resources that include programs specific to gay youth.

By 1996, the Metropolitan Atlanta Community Foundation (404-688-5525) will have distributed more than $100,000 in grant funds to local organizations for use exclusively for gay youth programs, excluding AIDS/HIV support, which is addressed extensively by numerous other local agencies, primarily Grady's Infectious Disease Clinic for Pediatrics and Adolescents (404-616-9796) and Positive Impact (404-885-9040). Some of the agencies with gay youth programs include: The Bridge (404-792-0070), a residential facility for troubled youth; Korean Community Service Center (404-936-0969), for Asian Pacific Islander youth; Feminist Women's Health Center (404-875-7115), a support group for young lesbians; Atlanta Parents, Friends and Family of Lesbians and Gays (404-875-9440), for local efforts on Project Open Mind, a campaign to fight hate and intolerance against gay children; and Latinos in Action (404-621-5743), a program offering shelter, counseling, and support for displaced and disadvantaged Latino gay youth.

Displaying little of the gender separatism that percolates through other large cities, lesbians and gay men mix pleasantly in queer restaurants, health clubs, bookstores, theaters, and they dance side by side in bars and clubs. Lesbian invisibility is as much a factor in Atlanta as in other cities, though the nearby Decatur/Emory area remains a lesbian enclave. Many of these women spearhead local activities, organizations, and awareness services on a range of issues: substance abuse, domestic violence, AIDS, breast cancer, self-esteem, education, parenting, politics, spirituality, housing, and social outreach.

Like a big extended Southern family, Atlanta's gays and lesbians know the value of communication. An emerging queer film and media community here directs the arts community, and gay publications often scoop the city's lackluster daily newspaper. Gays and lesbians also devote energy to every local fund-raising benefit, not just those that are AIDS-related.

The organizational gay or lesbian feels right at home in this uber-corporate city. The easiest way to clear a room or cause eyes to glaze over is, in fact, to hint that this urbane, temperate metropolis might have some problems, especially concerning the quality of life for queers.

But, while Atlanta is certainly much more relaxed in its political atmosphere than other Southern cities, gays and lesbians here have been victims of homophobia. The flashpoint occurred in 1993, when county commissioners in the suburban Atlanta community of Cobb County passed anti-gay resolutions legitimizing discrimination and encouraging attacks on its gay and lesbian residents. Atlanta's queer community rallied, however, and worked to find solutions to hate and ignorance-based problems.

Yet, it remains to be seen what will become of some of the city's tireless queer activists, whose numbers dwindle every year. Some flee to academia, others into professional health care and social work. Still, a few remain persistent warriors, like the handful who convinced Olympic organizers that Cobb County was not a sporting venue. That same group also forced the police to investigate a hideous string of gay murders in 1995 in midtown, and they continue to rally in front of City Hall demanding to know why gay adult bookstores—whose patrons more often than not include incognito suburban housewives and pillars of the community—and the vulnerable homeless remain targets of pre-Olympic police sting operations, while suburban and inner-city crime rates soar.

Despite Georgia's antiquated sodomy laws, Cobb County's biblically impaired bigots, and the city's solipsistic, self-promotion hoopla, queer Atlanta stands apart from the populace by energetically combining moonlight and magnolias with free-wheeling fun. Atlanta enjoys one of the nation's largest Pride Day celebrations every June, and a growing gay Black Pride celebration. The annual August Hot 'Lanta weekend ranks right at the top of the gay men's red-hot party circuit.

In less than two decades, Atlanta has exponentially increased its population and expanded its parameters with a dizzying web of freeways. In doing so, it has isolated some groups and become frighteningly expensive and high maintenance for all. Irrespective of its prosperity and genuine racial harmony, Atlanta is a city once described by a former mayor as "perpetually a teenaged boy."

This is very much a young city struggling with its identity, which encompasses convention-pleasing strip clubs, a burgeoning music scene, uneven professional sports teams, cookie-cutter suburbs, and, increasingly, an active and open gay and lesbian community.

MARGARET MAREE is an Atlanta native with more than fifteen years writing, producing, and reporting for print and broadcast journalism. In 1993, Maree organized the Atlanta chapter of the National Lesbian and Gay Journalists Association.

WE ARE FAMILY?: DIFFERENCES IN THE GAY COMMUNITY

When we first start to become involved with the gay community, many of us feel as if we are finally coming home after a long absence. We are meeting other people with whom we share something and who understand some of our concerns. But it can come as a surprise, then, when we join a group and realize that there are often struggles within our own community that concern our political and social agenda.

Yet, as gay people, no matter what sex, race, or religion we are, we all have something in common—we are gay. We all have similar concerns, such as working for equal rights, greater protection and antidiscrimination laws, and simply the right to live happily as lesbian, bisexual, transgendered, and gay people. But people also have problems, concerns, desires, and needs based on who they are as individuals. The gay community is made up of people from all walks of life, and every person brings her or his own thoughts and feelings into discussions about what the community needs to do, which issues are most important, and how things should be done.

For example, there are many people in the gay community who think that AIDS is the greatest problem facing us today. These people believe that we should all concentrate on finding a cure for AIDS, fighting for more money to combat AIDS, and letting the government know we are unsatisfied with the way the battle against AIDS is going. The people who believe this have many reasons for believing it. Many of them have AIDS or are living with HIV, the virus believed to cause AIDS. Many of them have lost friends, lovers, or family members to AIDS.

But other people think other things are more important. Women and men with children, for example, may be most concerned with getting laws changed so that it is not illegal for gay people to adopt children or to keep children in cases of divorce. Each year many lesbians die from breast cancer and other cancers, yet little or no research has been done on how lesbians are affected by cancer as a group. To many people, this is just as important, if not more important, than finding a cure for AIDS or getting the right to adopt children. People who have been fired for being gay think that job security is the most important thing.

The problem comes when we ignore the concerns of other people and say that one thing is more important than another. It's easy for us to ignore problems when we ourselves aren't going through them and probably won't go through them. But ignoring other people's problems, or saying that they aren't as important as our own, only makes the differences between us wider. It's important that you begin now to try and understand the different needs of people in the gay community. That way, you have a head start on other people and you will have a better understanding of what it is to be part of the gay family.

What we need to concentrate on as gay people is how we can bring our community together so that people support each other and work together to get things done. Even if something seems totally unimportant to you, just helping out a little bit, or simply lending encouragement to others who are concerned about the issue will strengthen the feeling that we are all working together. Then, when it comes time for getting support for your concerns, hopefully people will be there to help you too.

When you first start becoming active in the gay community, you may become frustrated. You may feel as though people just don't care enough or work hard enough to build a community. Or you might feel that your concerns are not being taken seriously. If this happens, try to remember that just because all of us are gay doesn't mean everyone gets along. In fact, it can often mean the opposite. Imagine if all of a sudden a lot of different people with different backgrounds and different lives are put into one room and told that they're now all part of the same family and have to work together. That's what being part of the gay community is like.

As you become more and more involved in the gay community, try to pay attention to the different kinds of people you meet. Listen to what they have to say and find out about who they are. For many years, gay people formed groups based on what their particular concern was. For example, African-American lesbians formed groups with other African-American lesbians, and gay veterans formed communities with other gay veterans and so on. Some of these groups have accomplished a lot and still do so.

But it's also important to reach out to other people and try to understand them, to listen to their stories and learn what you have in common as gay people. Gay organizations have failed too often because the different groups have fought about whose issues should be taken care of first. As young gay people, you have the opportunity to change the way the gay community works. As you get older, you will be taking over leadership roles in gay politics, in gay organizations, and in gay causes. By learning early on how to work with people who might be different from yourself, by learning to listen and to accept other people's ideas and concerns, you will be able to make great changes in the lives of gay people.

As you become more involved in the gay world, be on the lookout for ways in which you can meet more gay people, people who might not be just like you. Find out about all the different kinds of issues that gay people are fighting for, issues like the rights of gay people in other countries, AIDS issues and other health issues, lesbian issues, issues for older gay people, veterans' issues, adoption issues, rights issues. Ask questions and see where you can get involved. Because the more you do, the more you will start to make a difference in the lives of the next generation of gay people.

The following books contain writing about the experience of being gay or lesbian and a person of color.

BEAM, JOSEPH, ed., *In the Life: A Black Gay Anthology* (Boston: Alyson Publications, 1986).

GÓMEZ, ALMA, CHERRIÉ MORAGA AND MARIANNE ROMO-CARMONA, *Cuentos: Stories by Latinas* (Latham, NY: Kitchen Table: Women of Color Press, 1983).

HEMPHILL, ESSEX, ed., *Brother to Brother: New Writings by Black Gay Men* (Boston: Alyson Publications, 1991).

LEONG, RUSSELL, ed., *Asian American Sexualities: Dimensions of the Gay and Lesbian Experience* (New York: Routledge, 1995).

LIM-HING, SHARONE, ed., *The Very Inside: An Anthology of Writing by Asian and Pacific Islander Lesbian and Bisexual Women* (Toronto: Sister Vision, 1994).

MCKINLEY, CATHERINE AND L. JOYCE DELANEY, *Afrekete: An Anthology of Black Lesbian Writing* (New York: Anchor, 1995).

RAMOS, JUANITA, ed., *Compañeras: Latina Lesbians* (New York: Routledge, 1994).

ROSCOE, WILL, ed., *Living the Spirit: A Gay American Indian Anthology* (New York: St. Martin's Press, 1989).

SILVERA, MAKEDA, ed., *Piece of My Heart: A Lesbians of Colour Anthology* (Toronto: Sister Vision, 1991).

SMITH, BARBARA, ed., *Home Girls: A Black Feminist Anthology* (Latham, NY: Kitchen Table: Women of Color Press, 1983).

TRUSILLO, CARLA, *Chicana Lesbians: The Girls Our Mothers Warned Us About* (Berkeley, CA: Third Woman's Press, 1991).

WILLIAMS, WALTER L., *The Spirit and the Flesh: Sexual Diversity in American Indian Culture* (Boston: Beacon Press, 1992).

STEPHEN GENDEL: NEWS REPORTER, CNBC

Millions of people around the country see Stephen Gendel on television every day, often several times a day. As the chief medical correspondent for cable channel CNBC, he covers stories about all kinds of health-related topics. He also regularly fills in as the host of the live talk show *Rivera Live*, where he gained wide exposure for his coverage of many different aspects of the O.J. Simpson murder trial. And he hosts a biweekly show about the criminal justice system called *On Trial*, examining various high-profile court cases from a variety of angles. In 1993, Stephen surprised many viewers when he came out as a gay man on air during the talk show *Real Personal*, becoming one of only a handful of openly gay reporters on national television.

Being an out public figure is a far cry from Stephen's early life. Married for many years, he raised four daughters before coming out as a gay man. "I tried so hard to be straight," he says. "I tried to convince myself that the feelings I had for other men just meant that I had a broader spectrum of sexuality than most other people. I could not bring myself to admit that I was gay for a long, long time." During this time, he suffered from depression and horrible feelings of guilt. "It was really awful," he says of those years. "I was not a very nice person. I became very driven to succeed. I was very angry. I worked as hard as I could and made everybody around me miserable in my attempt to forget about what I was feeling."

When he did come out, Stephen faced other difficulties. "I had no idea what to do next," he recalls. "After all those years of living as a straight man, I didn't even know how to begin meeting other gay people or living as a gay person. I had spent so long avoiding the gay community that I had no idea how to find it." Stephen came out to a coworker, who began to introduce him to other gay people, and slowly he started to form a new network of friends within the gay community. One event in particular stands out in his memory. "There was a straight woman at work who every year held a Thanksgiving

dinner for all of the gay people in the office," he remembers. "The year I came out I went to the dinner and was the greeter at the door. I will never as long as I live forget the sight of all of those jaws dropping as I opened the door to let people in. All of these people who knew me as being straight couldn't believe I had come out. That dinner really showed me the importance of gay family and the strength of the gay community."

When he went to work for CNBC, Stephen was informally out to coworkers, but had never come out publicly. Then one day a producer for *Real Personal* asked him to be a guest on a show about gay issues. "It was a very intense moment for me," he says. "As a reporter, I'm not supposed to bring my own issues and feelings into the stories I report. But at the same time, I felt it was something important to talk about. I think it really helps people to understand issues when they see the people those issues affect. I decided that coming out might help people realize that they did know someone who was gay, and that maybe that would help them begin to understand what gay people are about."

After coming out, Stephen says he felt wonderful. "It was such a freeing experience," he recalls. "When you are open about something like that, then nothing can hurt you. If everyone knows, you have nothing to hide." Being out also allowed him to work on some stories of personal interest. During celebrations for the twenty-fifth anniversary of the Stonewall Riots, Stephen was able to report on the event. "That was great," he says. "It felt really wonderful as a gay person to be talking about the history of my community. I felt very proud to be doing that."

Stephen says that the real impact of being out at work came after the death of his lover, Joseph, from heart failure in 1995. "Joseph's death really made me see how wonderful it is to be out," he says. "Everyone at work knew what happened, and they were all very supportive. If I was still in the closet, I wouldn't have had any of that support. I

wouldn't have been able to tell anyone what happened. I wouldn't have been able to grieve for him. I probably wouldn't even have been able to get time off."

While Stephen says that being out as a gay person might possibly prevent him from being considered for certain jobs, he has no regrets about coming out. "Reporters don't really talk about their personal lives on air," he says, "so most people don't know who is gay and who isn't. There are a few of us who are out, and a lot more who aren't out. But there are many gay and lesbian people in the industry, from producers and writers to sportscasters and anchorpeople. The more people come out, the more it won't be a big deal."

Most important, he feels, is what he can accomplish by being honest about himself. "What I hope it does," he says, "is show people that we are out here. I hope people knowing that the person giving them the news is gay will make them realize that a lot of other people they know could be gay too. I especially hope that my being out can help other gay people, who might be in the closet and hurting like I was, understand that there is another way to live. The best thing for me is getting letters from people who say knowing that I'm gay too has helped them accept themselves."

WHY DO SOME PEOPLE HATE US?: HOMOPHOBIA

As most of us are all too aware, there are some people who do not like gay people. We read about gay people being attacked by gay-bashers; we hear congresspeople on television talk about not giving "special rights" to gays; we hear people say that they want to beat up faggots or show dykes "how to do it right." This kind of behavior is homophobia, which is any kind of verbal or physical abuse aimed at gay people.

Homophobia can be as simple as referring to someone as a "faggot" in a conversation, or not giving someone a job because you think she's a lesbian. Or it can be something more visible, like beating up or killing someone because he's gay, or not letting a parent in a divorce case have visitation rights because she is a lesbian. Homophobia takes many forms, some of them very obvious and some of them completely invisible. Whatever form it takes, homophobia is painful and hurtful.

Unfortunately, homophobia is a big problem. We live in a country where everyone is supposed to be equal under the law. We don't like to think that people can do horrible things to us just because they don't like us. But the sad truth is that, all too often, they can. Hundreds of gay women and men are beaten up and killed every year, just because someone doesn't like them. More are injured in far less obvious ways. There are entire political campaigns backed by millions of dollars just to get laws passed that say that gay people cannot have equal protection and equal rights. There are whole organizations established to "warn" the American people about gays. The armed services has fought a long battle to keep gays out of the military despite years and years of evidence that gay people make just as good or even better soldiers than straight people. Whether we like it or not, whether it's fair or not, homophobia is everywhere, and we have to learn how to deal with it. We also have to learn how not to let homophobia prevent us from living proudly and happily as gay people.

The word *homophobia* says it all. *Phobia* means "a fear of." Homophobia is the fear of homosexuals. It is a *fear*, not an anger or a hatred. The anger and hatred come because people are afraid, but it all starts with a fear.

It sounds silly, someone being afraid of homosexuals. But think about it. Whenever you see someone talking negatively about gay people, what are they usually doing? They're shouting. Their faces are red and angry, their mouths are open, and their fingers are pointing and shaking. Sometimes they're waving signs or clenching their fists. Whatever they're doing, they always look afraid. They look as though they're trying to protect themselves from something that can hurt them.

But have you ever thought about *why* these people are afraid of gays? After all, there has to be some really good reason why they're all so angry at us, right? Wrong. In fact, some of the most homophobic people in the world have never even met a gay person, at least as far as they know. Their homophobia is based entirely on some strange concept of what they *think* homosexuals are.

So, what do they think we are? Well, most of them aren't even sure. Some of them just say we're perverts who go against God's teachings. Some of them say we're the cause of AIDS, without really knowing anything about how AIDS is caused or how it's spread. Some of them say we're these really scary people who want to take over the world and make everyone just like us.

Many times the issue comes down to children. For some reason, homophobic people are convinced that all gay people want to molest children or else "make" children gay. They think that just by being around us or just by knowing about us that all children will want to be gay too, just like they might want to be firemen or astronauts if they visit a firehouse or space center.

The truth is that about 98 percent of all child molesters are heterosexual men. Tell that to a homophobe and he'll probably argue back and forth all night about it; but the truth is that gay people very, very seldom molest children. The few who do have psychological problems that have nothing to do with being gay, just as heterosexual child molesters have psychological problems that have nothing to do with being straight.

What people are really afraid of when it comes to children, and even when it comes to themselves, is that being around gay people or even just knowing that gay people exist will give other people the message that it's OK to be gay. They are afraid that seeing that there are happy gay people will make young people understand that what they might be feeling is perfectly acceptable and normal. They're afraid that seeing gay people will give young people the courage to express themselves as gays if that's what they are. They think that if they "protect" children from gays, that children will grow up straight because they won't know that gays even exist.

But why are people afraid of homosexuality at all? That's where it gets interesting, because it's almost all about sex. When most people say that homosexuality is disgusting, what are they really saying? Usually they're saying that homosexual *sex* is disgusting. After all, to most people, what makes us gay is the fact that we are attracted to people of the same sex. That's it. That's all they "know" about being gay.

People seem to think that people are gay because they like the kind of sex that gay people have. In fact, some religious groups say that it's fine for a person to be homosexual and to have homosexual thoughts, as long as he or she doesn't actually act on those feelings and have sex with someone of the same sex. In other words, if a man who is gay marries a woman, he can have all the gay thoughts he wants to as long as he doesn't actually have sex with another man. According to these people, it's the physical sex that makes us gay.

The reality is that gay people like gay sex because they like the people they're having it with. You want to make love with a person because you're attracted to that person. When you analyze it, and we will in a later chapter, people pretty much have the same kind of sex whether they're gay or straight. So to say that someone decides to be lesbian or gay because she or he really loves to have lesbian or gay sex is pretty funny. Would anyone really go through all of the things gay people have to go through in this world just to have a certain kind of sex?

When it comes right down to it, most people are afraid of gay people because they don't want to think that they themselves might be in any way gay. This doesn't mean that all homophobic men are really gay, or that all homophobic women are really lesbians, although a surprising number of them are. What it means is that homophobic people are afraid of the *possibility* that they could be gay.

Yet, knowing that homophobia is caused by fear and ignorance doesn't make it any easier to feel better when someone calls us names just to be mean, or when they hurt us physically. But it does help us to understand why people act the ways they do, and understanding is the first step toward change. By understanding why people are afraid of us, we can begin to try and change the way people see us and the way we see ourselves.

DEALING WITH HOMOPHOBIA

Why should we be concerned about homophobia? After all, unless we are actually the victims of it, it's a lot easier to ignore it and keep ourselves safely away from it.

But there are important reasons why all of us have to be aware of homophobia and know how to confront it. The most obvious reason is because homophobia can lead to violence. Many gay people have been beaten up or killed because we are gay or because someone thinks that we are gay. In the past few years alone, a lesbian woman and her gay male roommate were burned to death when gay-bashers threw a homemade bomb through the window of their home, two lesbians in Tennessee have repeatedly had people shoot at their home and threaten to kill them for being gays, and a young Navy seaman was beaten and kicked to death by several of his own shipmates because he was gay.

As gay people become more and more visible, and gay issues are more in the news, violence against homosexuals increases. People want us to stay silent and hidden, because that way they can pretend that we really don't exist. As more and more gay people stand up for their rights, it makes everyone realize just how many of us there are, and this makes them upset. People who are homophobic often look for people on whom to vent their anger and frustration, and too often their victims are simply in the wrong place at the wrong time.

Some states and cities have laws that make it illegal to hurt people who are gay. These are called "hate crime" laws, because the crimes are committed simply out of hate and not for any other motivation, such as robbery or gang fighting. But these laws are often hard to enforce, because the people who commit hate crimes certainly aren't going to admit that they attacked or killed someone just because she is a lesbian, or just because he was coming out of a gay bar. It takes a lot of time to prove that a crime was motivated by hate, and most police departments are not willing to take the time.

And while some law enforcement people are helpful and compassionate regarding gay-bashings, many others are not. Many victims of hate crimes report being further teased or ridiculed by the police when they try to report the crimes. This makes it difficult for gay people to report these crimes against them. If someone feels that she or he is going to be ridiculed for being gay, especially for being attacked for being gay, the chances are that a crime will go unreported. No one wants to report what is already a traumatic and sometimes embarrassing incident if the people he is reporting it to make him feel even worse. And even if a hate crime is reported and the criminal is caught, that doesn't ease the mental and physical pain of being attacked simply for being gay. For some people, it seems easier just to remain silent.

Gay-bashing is a very visible form of homophobia. But not all homophobia is so obvious. While the effects of gay-bashing can be seen in the bruises and cuts on a person's body, other scars from homophobia are less visible. All over the country, people are voting on laws that will, for example, give gay people equal protection and equal rights in matters of housing, jobs, adoption, health benefits. While these issues seem perfectly reasonable to us, many homophobic people want these laws overturned or rejected. Many even want there to be laws saying that gay people *can't* have equal rights. The most visible example of this is the ongoing campaign in Colorado, where homophobic groups have been campaigning fiercely and using all kinds of lies, distortions, and fear tactics to make people vote for laws making it illegal to give equal rights to gay people. But thanks to efforts by local gay groups, these laws have not been voted in. Still, it gets harder and harder each year to fight against the hatred and the fear caused by homophobia.

It's very easy for most of us to think that this doesn't affect us. After all, we might think, how many gay people really want to adopt children? And how many gay people really want to be in the military? The answer is that enough do so that it should matter to all of us. If even one person wants to adopt a child and is told no, that's enough reason for all of us to care. And the reason it's enough is because when we let people tell us we aren't worth fighting for, it lets them keep believing that we aren't people who deserve equal rights and equal respect. If we let people take away or deny us even the smallest right, then we let them tell us that we aren't worth enough as people to have that right. But if we stand up and say, "No, we deserve the right to adopt children," or, "We have every right to defend our country," then we make the people who say we can't do those things see that we will not be treated badly, that we respect ourselves and other gay people enough to demand that we be treated fairly.

Besides legal rights and the threat of physical abuse, one of the biggest reasons homophobia is an important issue is because it prevents people from accepting themselves. Gay people often have trouble accepting themselves because they know there are people who will not like them simply because they're lesbian, bisexual, transgendered, or gay. If someone grows up hearing nothing but horrible things about homosexuals, that person is going to have very negative feelings about gay people. The chances are that person will also grow up to be homophobic. If that person is gay herself, then she is going to have an incredibly bad self-image, because she will have been taught to hate what she herself is, and it will be very hard for her to accept herself as a gay person. But if she sees that there are millions of gay women and men who demand equal rights and equal respect, then perhaps she will start to see that what she has been taught is wrong, that she is a person who has a lot to offer the world and who deserves happiness.

Even gay people can be homophobic. How? We can be homophobic by hating ourselves, by being ashamed of who we are and not wanting anyone to know us. We can be homophobic by refusing to admit our own gayness and refusing to let ourselves be happy the way we are. We can be homophobic by letting other people get away with saying horrible things about gay people, or by not informing ourselves about gay issues. We can be homophobic by saying things that are unkind about other gay people, such as belittling people for acting "too gay" or for being "too out" about who they are. Whenever we say that certain kinds of gay people don't belong in our community just because they aren't like us or because we are embarrassed by them, we are being homophobic.

How do we fight homophobia? Luckily, there are many ways. Fighting homophobia can mean stopping our friends when they start to say negative things about gays or start telling jokes about us. It can mean giving friends or family members a book about gay people so that they can start to educate themselves. It can mean joining or supporting a group that actively fights homophobia, such as the Lesbian and Gay Anti-Violence Project, which monitors anti-gay attacks and police response to them, or the Gay and Lesbian Alliance Against Discrimination (GLAAD), which monitors the media for anti-gay movies, television programs, radio shows, and print references.

Another excellent way to fight homophobia is to make yourself heard. This means calling or writing letters to companies who support gay-positive television programs, advertising campaigns, or causes. This is a tool used very effectively by anti-gay forces, who have successfully prevented a number of gay-positive television programs and advertising campaigns from appearing by threatening to boycott the companies who advertise on the shows. By applying consumer pressure, people can greatly influence how a company spends its advertising dollars. If a company thinks that they will lose sales by offending a group of people, more often than not they will do what that group wants them to.

For example, when the television show *Roseanne* aired an episode in which Roseanne and a lesbian character kiss, many advertisers were besieged with telephone calls from anti-gay people demanding that they not buy commercial time during the program. The same happened when NBC aired *Serving in Silence: The Margarethe Cammermeyer Story.* Some companies did pull their commercials; others did not. Interestingly, those companies that did air commercials reported that they received many angry letters and telephone calls, but very few supportive ones from gays and lesbians.

One way to make a positive difference is to write or call companies that do sponsor gay-positive television programs or movies and thank them for their support. If companies think that they are earning the trust of a group of people who can potentially spend money on their products, they are going to continue to be supportive. However, if they think that the community doesn't care, they probably won't bother. Conversely, if you write to companies that sponsor or support anti-gay programs, and let them know that you will be taking your business elsewhere because of their actions, you may help convince them to alter their spending patterns.

All of these things can go a long way toward fighting homophobia. They may also be more than you can do right now. Many of us feel that we can't tell our families about ourselves yet, and don't feel comfortable joining a gay group. There's nothing wrong with that. That's just the reality of homophobia.

One thing we can *all* do to fight homophobia, no matter where we live or who we are, is start to think of ourselves, and all gay people, as worthy of respect. If every gay person in the world really believed that she or he deserved equal rights and equal respect, then we would have an unbeatably strong family that would make amazing changes. But as long as we hide and let other people treat us badly, we will not be able to fight effectively for our rights.

How do you do this? There are many things you can do. You can educate yourself about gay issues. Find out if your state or city has laws protecting the rights of gay people. Find out if your city has hate crime laws that punish people who attack gays. Find out if gay people in your state can adopt children. How do you find out? Go to the library and ask how to look up information on state and local laws, or call a local lesbian and gay community center. Many centers are meeting places for political action groups.

If there are presidential, congressional, or local political elections coming up, find out what the candidates think about these issues. Read newspapers and listen to the evening news to see what the candidates running for office think, not just about gay issues but about all kinds of issues. Because the more you know now, the better prepared you will be to really start making a difference in the way things work.

Another thing you can do is to remember that no matter what anyone may say or do to you, you are a valuable person. The way homophobia gets to us is by making us feel ashamed, embarrassed, or angry about being gay. It's very easy to be intimidated by homophobia. We start to think that people are picking on us because something *is* wrong with us. The truth is, there's something wrong with them. If someone feels the need to tease or hurt someone else just for being different, that person is sick.

But if you are the victim of homophobia, then what do you do? First, don't let yourself react to someone who taunts you, because that is exactly what she wants you to do. Walk away if you can, because words only mean what you think they mean. But if the abuse becomes physical, then you have several options, none of which is easy. You can always fight back. But remember—physical violence almost always leads to more and more violence, and it doesn't solve the problem, at least not in the long run.

However, one positive option is to take self-defense classes. Self-defense, including the martial arts, is not fighting. It is a way to avoid fighting by making it impossible for people to attack you. You learn to block attacks and how to disarm punches, kicks, and other blows your attacker may try to use against you. Martial arts are based on spiritual principles about nonviolence, and they are excellent ways both to exercise and to learn self-control and self-protection. Many gyms, YMCAs, YWCAs, and community centers teach self-defense classes, and there are many private schools teaching all kinds of martial arts and self-defense techniques. These are good classes for *anyone* to take, and knowing a few smart moves could easily prevent an attack.

If you are the victim of a serious gay-bashing incident, where you or someone else is hurt badly, then you should report it to the police. If you are afraid to go to the police, then I suggest you call a local lesbian and gay community services center or one of the groups listed in the resource section of this book. Groups such as the Lesbian and Gay Anti-Violence Project in New York City can help you and tell you where you can report the crime to people who will listen to you and be respectful and helpful. If you don't have such a group in your area, then you should tell a trusted friend or someone who can help you go to the police.

If you are the victim of gay-bashing, and you feel that there is not a single person around you that you can tell about it, call one of the hotlines set up for gay people. These are anonymous, and the people

10 THINGS YOU CAN DO TO FIGHT HOMOPHOBIA

1. **KEEP INFORMED** on gay issues

2. **FIND OUT** what your local school's position is on teaching about gay issues and gay people; join the school board

3. **SUPPORT AND CAMPAIGN** for gay-positive political leaders

4. **ORGANIZE** a gay neighborhood watch or patrol to discourage anti-gay activities

5. **DON'T BUY** records or books by anti-gay artists

6. **ASK** television producers to include positive gay characters on their shows

7. **DON'T PATRONIZE** stores or restaurants with anti-gay policies

8. **VOLUNTEER** at a gay anti-violence project

9. **SUPPORT** gay rights organizations by volunteering or making a donation

10. **PATRONIZE** credit card companies and long-distance telephone services that donate to gay causes

who answer the phones are there to help you and listen to you. As painful as it may be to talk about, keeping it inside will only make it worse.

Homophobia can be very, very scary. It can be so scary that we start to think that we will never let ourselves be active gay people because someone might hurt us. That's what homophobes want us to think. They want us to be so scared that we shut up. They want us to be so scared that we stay invisible. They want us to be afraid of them.

We can beat homophobes and homophobia by standing up to that fear. Yes, it's OK to be afraid. Sometimes it's even OK to run away. But every time we stand up to an incidence of homophobia—every time we refuse to laugh at a homophobic joke, refuse to eat at a restaurant that won't hire gay people, are kind to someone who has experienced homophobia—we make the power of homophobia that much weaker.

NEW YORK, NEW YORK — Michael Thomas Ford

New York City is probably the easiest place in the United States to be gay. Along with San Francisco, New York is the city most people think about when they think about where gay people live. New York has its own gay neighborhoods, restaurants, bars, newspapers, stores, and anything else gay you can think of. New York is the place where the modern gay rights movement began, and every year one of the largest Gay Pride celebrations takes place here on the last weekend of June, where hundreds of thousands of women and men hold a big party with dances, rallies, and parades. For many gay people, living in New York seems like the ultimate dream.

Despite all of these things, it can be difficult for someone unfamiliar with New York's gay community to find it and become part of it. All of the different choices available to gay people in New York can be the very thing that makes it hard for someone to decide where to begin.

New York has one of the oldest lesbian and gay community centers in the country, and this is a great place to start for someone looking to find out more about New York's huge gay community. Called simply "the center" by the local gay community, the Lesbian and Gay Community Services Center at 208 West 13th Street (212-620-7310) provides a meeting place for hundreds of different groups ranging from gay police officers to bisexuals, gay parents to Asian-American lesbians. The center prints a schedule of events for each month, and the schedule also includes telephone contact numbers for each group that meets there. In addition, the center itself frequently holds orientation nights for people who have recently moved to New York and for those who want to become more involved in the gay community. It also sponsors many other events, from dances to writing workshops, support groups to social groups for children with gay parents.

In addition to the groups that meet at the center, there are hundreds of other groups that hold regular meetings around New York. New York's gay community supports an incredible range of social, political, and recreational groups, from gay runners to gay Democrats, gay school teachers to groups for transsexuals. Among many other things, New York also has a world famous Gay Men's Chorus, an active gay volleyball league, and groups for gay writers. There are lesbian martial arts clubs, gay African-American groups, and organizations for gay journalists.

New York's gay community is also a very political one, and there are numerous opportunities for people who want to become involved in that area. There are several lesbian and gay people on the city council, and gay issues are central in local elections. Groups including the International Lesbian and Gay Organization (ILGO) and the Gay and Lesbian Alliance Against Defamation (GLAAD) have offices here, and organizations like the Lesbian Avengers provide numerous opportunities for women and men who want to become involved in hands-on activism.

When I was trying to figure out how to become involved in the community here, I started by joining the membership committee at the center. From there I met many different people and joined several other groups. Before I knew it, I had established a wide circle of friends from many different areas. Many of the gay groups in the city are connected to each other in some way, and it isn't hard to find what you're looking for once you take that first step of buying a gay paper, going to the center, or attending any kind of meeting.

In addition to organized groups, New York's gay community also has a thriving social scene. There are dozens of bars and clubs specifically for lesbian and gay people, as well as theaters and bookstores that cater to gay people. A Different Light bookstore, New York's largest gay bookstore, frequently holds readings, as do many of the city's coffee shops and artists' spaces. Every night of the week there are many different things to choose from if you're looking for something fun to do. *Homo Xtra* ("H/X"), the city's weekly guide to gay entertainment, lists many different kinds of gay events and contains hundreds of ads for gay stores, restaurants, bars, and clubs, as do *The*

Native and *LGNY*, two of the city's gay newspapers. The *Village Voice* newspaper also contains listings of many different cultural events happening around the city, including plays, movies, art exhibits, lectures, and workshops of special interest to gay men and lesbians.

For young gay people, the Hetrick-Martin Institute at 2 Astor Place (212-674-2400) provides many different kinds of services, including social activities, counseling, and support groups. The institute also runs the Harvey Milk School, a high school for gay students who find it difficult to attend regular public schools. The institute is a wonderful place to begin exploring the many different things available for gay youth in New York.

New York is home to many colleges and universities as well, and most have their own gay groups. Columbia University has a large lesbian, gay, and bisexual student group, and often holds dances and other social events. New York University and Barnard College also have such groups. Even if you don't attend these schools, you can usually participate in their activities, and if you are a young person this is a great way to meet other gay young people in a pressure-free setting.

While the sheer size of the city and all that it offers can intimidate people, it can be a wonderful place to live as a gay person. New York has several thriving gay neighborhoods. Greenwich Village is probably the most famous gay neighborhood in the world, and today many gay men and lesbians still call it home. The Village contains dozens of gay restaurants, bars, clubs, and stores, and the population is diverse. While the Village is the center of the gay community, other neighborhoods popular with gay men include Chelsea on the west side of the city and Gramercy Park on the east side. The East Village is a funkier, grittier neighborhood, and home to both gay women and men into a more "alternative" scene. For lesbians and a growing number of gay men, the neighborhood of choice is Park Slope in Brooklyn, a quick subway or cab ride away from Manhattan.

New York offers more than any other city in the country in terms of things to do, convenience, and social life. But the city is far from being a paradise. New York is a very expensive place to live, especially the Village. It is very dirty and crowded. While gay people are certainly an integral part of life here, and seeing two men or women holding hands in public is not uncommon, gay-bashing and anti-gay activity is still a problem. And although the police in the city have improved relations with the gay community, many people still feel that anti-gay attacks are not taken very seriously.

Ironically, some of the things that are so great about being gay in New York are the same things that make it hard to be gay here. It would be nice to say that the gay community is one big happy family, but that isn't true. New York's gay community is made up of people from every possible background. This means that the community is very diverse, but it also means that it's sometimes harder to get people to agree on things. For example, gay men and lesbians seldom socialize or work together, and many people of color say that they don't feel at home in the larger gay community. Because there are so many different kinds of people with so many different issues and concerns, people tend to form both political and social groups around one particular issue instead of trying to work together to solve issues we all face. This means that there can be three or four groups all concerned with the same problem, but not working together or even aware of each other.

Because it is easy to be gay here, many people forget that the city is the exception to what it is like to be gay in America, not the rule. In fact, many gay people move here to get away from the pressures of the rest of the world. Living so easily is wonderful, but it can also be deceiving. While the gay community here has organized and accomplished great things concerning some issues, such as AIDS, many people complain that New Yorkers are far too complacent and uninterested in life outside New York.

Still, there is no denying that living as a gay person in New York is an amazing experience. New York offers many different opportunities for gay people of all kinds to be with other gay people and to explore their interests and their identities. Many of these opportunities don't exist anywhere else. Because there are so many places for gay people to be open about who we are in New York, many gay people come here because it's exciting to be surrounded by so many other openly gay people and to be involved in so many gay things.

YOU'RE OUT!

One of the biggest issues for many gay people, no matter how long we've been involved in the gay community, is how open we can be about our sexuality, to what extent we can let the people we are in contact with on a day-to-day basis know that we are gay. This is not a book about coming out or about how to come out. There are several of those already, especially Michelangelo Signorile's *Outing Yourself: How to Come Out as Lesbian or Gay to Your Family, Friends, and Coworkers*. But because being out is such a big part of being a member of the gay community, and because it is something we all struggle with, it is important to discuss it a little bit.

Coming out essentially means letting other people know that we are gay. When someone is secretive about her sexuality, and doesn't let anyone know she is a lesbian, we say that person is "in the closet," as though she were hiding inside a small room with no windows for anyone to see through. Someone who is in the closet does not want anyone to know that she's gay, and may even go out of her way to appear to be straight.

When that person decides that it is time to start letting her sexuality be an open issue, we say that she has come out of the closet, or opened the door to her hiding place and emerged into the world for everyone to see. She may still have some fears about being gay, and about people knowing that she's gay, but she is willing to let people know who she is. If someone asks you, "Are you out?" they are asking you if you have told anyone else that you are gay.

For a lot of us, the phrase "coming out" makes us panic. We think that coming out means painting the words I'M GAY across our foreheads and marching down the street. We think it means calling up every single person we know and telling them that we're gay, and starting off every conversation with everyone we meet by saying, "Hi, I'm gay." We think that by coming out we will be exposing ourselves to all kinds of horrible things and to all sorts of painful experiences. For many of us, just thinking about letting people know that we are gay is enough to make us feel nervous or sick. We feel as though there is no way in the world we could ever do it, and that we never will.

What is being out really all about? Coming out, just like accepting yourself, is a series of steps. Some of these steps will be small ones, like letting yourself think that it's OK for you to be lesbian or gay, buying a gay book, or wearing gay symbol earrings. Other events will be more significant, like telling your family about yourself or getting actively involved in a gay community center. Coming out can also be telling just one very important friend about yourself, or joining one gay group.

Coming out involves a lot of different things. Even just letting yourself think "I'm gay" or "I'm lesbian" is coming out. It's coming out to yourself, which is the first step. Once you develop love for yourself and an understanding of who you are as a gay person, then coming out in other ways is much easier.

Do you have to come out? No, because it's not always that easy to do so, and it's not a requirement for being gay, or even for being part of the gay community. Many women and men stay in the closet for years, some for their whole lives, because they can't bring themselves to come out. They believe it will upset their families, that their friends will feel ashamed, that they'll lose their jobs, and any number of other terrible things. They feel safe and secure inside the closet, where no one can harm them.

Are they really safe? In some ways they are. After all, if no one knows you're gay, then no one can hurt you for being gay. But staying in the closet has a hefty price tag attached to it. It takes a lot of effort to hide who you are. You have to be on guard constantly, watching what you say and what you do. You might invent girlfriends or boyfriends to cover up what you're really thinking and doing, or you might even force yourself to date straight people just so no one will suspect that you're gay. Staying in the closet means that you have no one to talk to about your concerns and feelings. It means you are alone.

While hiding your sexuality can make things easier for the moment, in the long run staying in the closet makes you feel guilty, ashamed, and unhappy. If you have to hide facets of your life, you will never be able to live freely. You can't talk about whom you're dating, what you do, or any of the things we usually like to tell our friends and families. You will feel like there's this big part of yourself that has to be hidden away from everyone because something bad *might* happen if you let people know who you really are.

Obviously, becoming involved in the gay community means you have to be out enough at least to admit to yourself that you're gay. But you can be involved in the gay community no matter how out you are. Donating money to a gay organization doesn't require you to be out at all; you just mail in a check. Attending a gay dance means you have to be willing at least to go where there are other gay people. Writing for a gay paper or campaigning for gay rights takes an added level of being out. The more out you are, the more things you can do and the more you can enjoy all that the gay community has to offer.

But don't feel that you can't become involved with the gay community because you aren't "out enough." Whatever stage you're at, you can lend your support to the community and enjoy some of the many different things the gay community offers. Just because you don't want people at work to know you're gay doesn't mean you can't attend gay plays or join a gay writers' group. Your parents don't have to know you're gay for you to be able to support a gay political candidate or volunteer at an AIDS organization.

In an ideal world, we would all be able to be out about our lives. But this isn't an ideal world. We are all at different places in our lives. As you become involved in the gay community, you will probably find yourself becoming more and more out. But even if you aren't as out as you'd like to be, or as others might like you to be, there is still a place for you in the community.

Gay young people have some special issues to face in regards to coming out. Young people are generally dependent on their families for financial support and for a place to live. If their parents react badly to their coming out, there is the possibility that they could make life very difficult. This can range from actually throwing a gay child out of the house to constantly making the young person feel bad about being gay or sending her or him to a psychiatrist, religious leader, or doctor to try to "cure" the homosexuality. Where an adult gay person can always choose to live away from her family or can somehow distance himself from a family that wants to make trouble for him, a gay young person has to live with the pressures of being out to a family she or he sees every day.

On the other hand, sometimes telling our parents can be the best thing we've ever done; certainly not the easiest, but the best. Well-informed and caring parents can help a gay young person immensely by supporting him and allowing him to be who he is without fear of having to hide. This can be an amazingly wonderful experience because it allows a young person to explore her feelings without the fear of being "found out" and without constantly having to hide a big part of her life from her family.

If you are a young person still living at home or still dependent upon your parents for support, whether or not you tell your parents is really up to you. What you have to consider is how telling your parents will affect *you,* not them. If you really believe that your parents, friends, and family will be supportive of you, and that your coming out will be a positive thing for your life (remember that positive doesn't always mean easy), then perhaps coming out as a gay person is right for you. But if you have reason to believe that your parents are going to react to finding out that you are queer by abusing you in any way, whether it's by actually throwing you out of the house, by telling you constantly that you're a horrible person who has disappointed and shamed them, or by telling you that you have to change who and what you are, then you might be better off waiting until you are in a situation where you do not have to be dependent upon them.

When we are afraid of coming out, no matter what age we are, it is because we are afraid of being rejected by the people we tell. We are afraid that our friends won't be our friends anymore or that our families won't love us anymore. We are afraid of disappointing our mothers and fathers. We are afraid of having to answer people's questions. We worry so much about these things that we forget why we want to come out in the first place, which is because we are proud of ourselves and of who we are as lesbian and gay people.

If you are trying to decide whether or not to come out, you should ask yourself why you want to come out and if you are prepared for what might happen when you come out. If you are doing it because you have accepted yourself as a gay person and you are ready for other people to know who you are as a person, then that's a good reason to come out. If you're doing it because someone else told you to, that's not a good reason. Think about how your life will be changed by coming out. If you are ready to take on those challenges, then you're probably ready to come out.

This doesn't mean you have to feel confident about every single part of your life; it just means that you understand who you are as a person and have decided that you are willing to share that person with other people because it will make you feel stronger about yourself.

If you are already out, you will probably still have some issues about how out you can be. This is normal. Some of us have no reservations about marching in a gay pride parade, but feel incredibly nervous about writing an article for a gay magazine with our name on it. Other people will willingly volunteer at a gay organization, but panic if someone asks them a question about gay issues at work. Some of us are out in some areas in our lives but not in other areas.

As you become more involved with the gay community, you will probably reach a number of points where you have to decide how out you can be about your sexuality. You might move from going to a gay support group to volunteering at an AIDS organization to demonstrating with a lesbian rights group. At each stage, you will have to ask yourself questions about how out you are willing to be. You might be one of the most active members in your school or community gay organization but still never have told your family about yourself. These are things most of us have faced at one time or another.

When you reach these points in your life, the important thing to ask yourself is how your being out will affect your life. How out we all should be is one of those issues that people within the community argue about constantly. Some people believe we all owe it to the community and to ourselves to be completely out. Others say it's an individual choice. Most people find that the more out they are, the better they feel about themselves. Certainly the more out you are, the more things you can do without worrying about who may find out. And the more out we all are, the more people in general will come to recognize that gay people are everywhere, which is certainly a positive thing.

10

GREAT BOOKS BY LESBIAN WRITERS: POETRY, NONFICTION, AND FICTION

1. *House Rules,* Heather Lewis
2. *Bastard Out of Carolina,* Dorothy Allison
3. *Stone Butch Blues,* Leslie Feinberg
4. *Oranges Are Not the Only Fruit,* Jeanette Winterson
5. *Rubyfruit Jungle,* Rita Mae Brown
6. *Zami: A New Spelling of My Name,* Audre Lorde
7. *Revolution of Little Girls,* Blanche McCrary Boyd
8. *Empathy,* Sarah Schulman
9. *S/he,* Minnie Bruce Pratt
10. *Normal Sex,* Linda Smukler

10

GREAT BOOKS BY GAY WRITERS: POETRY, NONFICTION, AND FICTION

1. *Safe As Houses,* Alex Jeffers
2. *Mysterious Skin,* Scott Heim
3. *Breaking the Surface,* Greg Louganis
4. *Becoming a Man,* Paul Monette
5. *The Naked Civil Servant,* Quentin Crisp
6. *Tales of the City,* Armistead Maupin
7. *Selected Poems of Langston Hughes,* Langston Hughes
8. *Dancing on Tisha B'Av,* Lev Raphael
9. *A Member of the Family,* edited by John Preston
10. *A Boy's Own Story,* Edmund White

DO I HAVE TO LIKE JUDY GARLAND?: THE TRUTH ABOUT STEREOTYPES

Whether we like to admit it or not, we often have preconceived ideas of what we think people are like or how we think they act simply because of who or what they are. These ideas are not firsthand but are based on things that we've heard, read, seen, or even imagined. Often these ideas are based on half-truths or misinformation.

There are also stereotypes, which are commonly accepted images of groups of people based on ignorance or on misunderstanding. You can usually tell a stereotype is coming when someone begins a sentence with the word *all*, as in "All Asians are good at math" or "All women are horrible drivers." Stereotypes are usually applied to whole groups of people and are used to make those groups look bad.

What kind of stereotypes are there about gay people? How about: lesbians hate men, gay men love *The Wizard of Oz*, lesbians look like men, gay men were smothered by their mothers, lesbians have short hair, gay men are effeminate, lesbians play softball, gay men adore Barbra Streisand, gay people take drugs, gay people are unhappy, gay men have AIDS, and the only thing gay people want to do is have sex.

Often we do not want to admit that there is anything true about a stereotype, especially if it is a stereotype about ourselves. Many books written for gay people point out that not all gay men look and act effeminate and that not all gay women look and act butch. We're told that the feminine man and the masculine woman are just stereotypes—false images that people who find us disgusting or upsetting put forth to make us look bad.

The danger in this thinking is that we ourselves often come to believe that those stereotypes are indeed bad. When I was growing up gay and afraid, these images were my worst nightmares. I was terrified that if I looked or acted even the least little bit feminine, everyone would know I

73

was gay. I worried about how I carried my books at school, how I threw a ball in gym class, and what clothes I wore. I worried about what kind of music I liked and what hobbies I had.

As I grew older, I developed an intense aversion to effeminate men, because I did not want to see myself in them or have them recognize me as being gay too. I thought that "queeny" men and "butch" women made all the "rest of us" look bad, that if they could just learn to look and act more "normal," everyone would leave the rest of us alone. I couldn't understand why anyone would ever want to act in a way that would make other people know what they were and possibly hate them. In fact, I would put down other people for being what I thought was too gay.

It is very hard for me to admit that I thought these things, and I am ashamed and embarrassed that I ever felt that way. But I think this aversion to these stereotypes is something that all of us go through on some level, whether it's directed at ourselves or at people around us. So many women I know spent years hiding behind dresses and makeup that they hated because they thought that if they could only look "less like lesbians" they would be left alone. And many men I know did the same kind of things, such as building up their bodies at the gym so that they could be one of the guys.

Hard as it is for me to believe now, I used to think that the men and women who appeared "straight" were the ones doing the gay community the most good. I thought they were the ones with the healthiest outlooks. *If we all acted like that,* I thought, *we wouldn't have any problems. We'd be just like everyone else.* Well, I was wrong. It's taken me a little time to learn this, but to be like everyone else isn't brave, and it isn't safe. It kills your spirit, and it hides what makes you the person you are. Fitting in by definition means making a compromise. It means changing to be more like your surroundings. It means deception.

The people in the gay community who do the most good are the ones who act like themselves.

Unfortunately, instead of being celebrated, these stereotypical are used against us to show us what other people think are the worst things about what we are. So, being a woman who looks masculine is bad, and so is being a man who likes to listen to show tunes. When those images are thrown at us again and again as weapons, we come to hate them, because seeing them makes us feel ashamed or frightened. Or we hate them because they really are what we are. Eventually, we start to defend ourselves by saying, "No, that's not what we are," when in fact it's often the case that we are those very things.

Every June, when many cities hold gay pride celebrations, television stations covering the events invariably show pictures of women in leather riding motorcycles and men dressed in drag, dancing in the streets. They show these pictures because the women and men in them are usually the most interesting things in the parades. They almost always have big smiles on their faces, and they wave and blow kisses at the cameras. It makes for good news. No one wants to see a bunch of ordinary people in shorts and T-shirts walking down a street holding signs. They want a spectacle.

A lot of people in the gay community wish these people weren't the ones shown on television. They would prefer to have pictures of people simply walking with signs asking for gay rights or more money for AIDS research. They would prefer it if the more "obvious" members of the gay community remained in the background so that people watching the parade on television don't get the wrong idea about gays and lesbians.

This makes sense. After all, most of us would like people to stop bothering us for being gay. We'd like them to understand that basically we're just like they are in that we want to be treated fairly and that we want the same rights and opportunities in life. What doesn't make sense is telling members of our own community that they make the rest of us look bad because they're being themselves. When we do that, we are being just as censorious and fearful as people who say all gays are bad people.

The fact is, there is no one way for gay people (or any people for that matter) to look or act. We come in all shapes and sizes and colors, which is one of the wonderful things about being part of such a diverse community. There are as many kinds of gay people as there are kinds of straight people.

The point is, if you fit one of the stereotypes used to describe gay people, that's great. And if you don't, that's great too. Don't run from who you are, because all you'll do in the long run is miss out on a lot of things you'll wish you'd done. Don't waste your time worrying about what people will think or say. You can take care of that when and if it happens. What's important is doing what makes you happiest. To pretend that stereotypes are a figment of straight people's imaginations, or to say that they are somehow embarrassing, is the worst kind of prejudice.

Imagine having to walk around all the time with a big sign around your neck saying I'M GAY. Women and men who fit the "stereotypical" images of what lesbians and gay men are have to face the world every single moment of their lives without protection. It seems to me that the bravest people in the world are the butch lesbians and the effeminate men who get called "dyke" and "faggot" for most of their lives. It takes a lot more courage for an obviously effeminate man to walk down the street past groups of other men, or for a butch woman to walk just about any-where, than it does to try and fit in with everyone else.

The 1969 Stonewall Riots in New York City, in which patrons of a gay bar called the Stonewall fought with police after one of their many raids, was the first really visible event of the modern gay rights movement. It is impor-tant to remember that the Stonewall Riots were led by a lot of drag queens, effeminate men, and bull dykes who were fed up with being harassed by the police for how they looked and acted. It was only after those "stereo-typical" gays picked up bottles, rocks, high heels, and sticks and started fighting for themselves that the more "normal" looking gays joined in.

Unfortunately, the struggle continues. And although all of us benefited from the Stonewall Riots, both straights and gays, still say, "Well, if she didn't look like that they wouldn't have attacked her" or "If he didn't act so queeny he wouldn't have gotten fired." It's easy to blame or hate peo-ple who fit stereotypes for bad things that happen to them. It's tempting to try and hide our true selves if we think that showing what we really are will make life harder.

But if we really want to be free as gay people, we have to be who we are, and that means accepting ourselves and others. It means fighting bigotry and hatred by allowing ourselves to do the things we want to do and looking the way we want to look. It means embracing stereotypes and turning them into images that make us proud, not ashamed.

What's important to remember is that there is no right or wrong way to be. What's wrong is when you try to change yourself simply because other people don't like what you are. What's right is learning to love who you are and giving yourself the freedom to explore different things. When you do that, then you are taking a giant step toward fighting homopho-bia and becoming the person you are inside.

1. RITES OF PASSAGE, Indigo Girls 2. YOUR LITTLE SECRET, Melissa Etheridge 3. INGÉNUE, k.d. lang 4. BE CAREFUL WHAT YOU WISH FOR..., Kristin Hall 5. PHANTOM CENTER, Ferron 6. WILLING TO WAIT, Melissa Ferrick 7. PLANTATION LULLABIES, Me'Shell NdegéOcello 8. WHALER, Sophie B. Hawkins 9. DISAPPEAR FEAR, disappear fear 10. PARANOID & SUNBURNT, Skunk Anansie

GREAT RECORDS BY FEMALE ARTISTS OR BANDS WITH OPENLY LESBIAN OR BISEXUAL MEMBERS

1. THE INNOCENTS, Erasure 2. CHEAPNESS AND BEAUTY, Boy George 3. DARE TO LOVE, Jimmy Somerville 4. VERY, The Pet Shop Boys 5. SOUTHPAW GRAMMAR, Morrissey 6. MONSTER, R.E.M. 7. MADE IN ENGLAND, Elton John 8. EUROFLAKE IN SILVERLAKE, Gregory Gray 9. COWBOYS AND ALIENS, Kitchens of Distinction 10. PILE UP, Pansy Division

GREAT RECORDS BY MALE ARTISTS OR BANDS WITH OPENLY GAY OR BISEXUAL MEMBERS

ROB ALLEN: POLICE OFFICER

Sergeant Rob Allen has been an officer with the Minneapolis Police Department for almost six years, working as a patrol officer and as a cycling instructor for the department's mountain bike division. In 1994, Rob came out as a gay man, one of the first openly gay officers on the force. Since then, he has become very involved in the gay community, and especially in improving communication between the gay community and the police department.

Accepting himself as a gay man and getting to the point where he could come out wasn't easy for Rob. Growing up, he had difficulty dealing with his feelings. "I really tried very hard not to be gay for way too long," he says. "I honestly feel that a dozen years of my life were wasted because I shied away from any meaningful relationships with people out of fear of being gay. I felt guilty about being dishonest with my friends. I made up relationships that didn't really exist to cover for myself. There's no worse feeling than that." Like many people, Rob even considered suicide at one point. "There was a period of my life where I was suicidal because I thought it would be easier to just end it than to come out. There was a point at which I actually bought a gun."

Luckily, Rob read a column his minister had written for the church bulletin about what he would do if he found out his son was gay. "It was a very positive message that he wrote," Rob remembers. "That more than anything made me see that it was worth living. It lifted me through the depression and despair. The Rock River in southern Wisconsin has a pistol in it as a result of that article."

After spending five years in the hotel industry, Rob decided it was time to fulfill his lifelong dream of becoming a police officer. Still closeted, he found hiding his sexuality to be a real strain. But it was dealing with some of the situations he faced as an officer that prompted him to come out." I had an interesting experience while I was struggling with whether or not to come out," he recalls. "I was called to a fight at a gay and lesbian youth center. There was a young lesbian woman in her teens who was very hostile, very hysterical, threatening us and so forth. She was accusing us of taking police action against her just because she was a lesbian. I looked back at her and said, 'Hey, I'm gay. This isn't a gay thing.' She immediately calmed down. My partner at the time assumed I was pretending to be gay just to calm her down. Later on we were talking about it, and he said it wouldn't matter to him if I was gay. So that was one thing that really furthered my decision to come out. The other thing that really pushed me was realizing that you really need to have out gay cops so that people start to see us and to understand what we're about, to eliminate that sense of hostility that exists between gay people and the police. When I saw the sense of calm that came over that young woman and the hostility that existed just because we were wearing blue shirts and badges disappear just because I was gay, that had a lot of impact on me."

After two other officers on the force came out, Rob decided that it was time for him to take the next step too. To his surprise, he and the other gay officers were readily accepted by their fellow officers. "My coming out went over much better than I thought it would," he says. "When I first started, I remember hearing somebody say that he'd feel really sorry for the first gay officer to come out on the force because he or she would be harassed. But that didn't happen. We've had a very positive experience. I had a perception of police culture that it wasn't acceptable to be gay. I haven't had any problems. I've found out how really great my friends were."

Rob's life also improved outside of work after coming out. "Being out has really improved my life. I came out to family, friends, and at work in the same week. Psychologically I am a much happier person now. I deal with stress better. I think I was probably clinically depressed before I came out, and I have no problems with that now. Being out makes me a far better police officer, and it makes me a better person too. Life is so much easier now. I'm involved in a committed relationship now, which was never a possibility for me before. So coming out freed me up to do so many other things. In fact, meeting my partner and realizing that this is what love can be is part of what encouraged me to come out."

His openness also allowed him to become involved in the Minneapolis gay community. "I went from zero involvement in the gay community to being the poster child for gay issues. I go to meetings of gay organizations now. I'm developing all kinds of friends in the community. It's opened up a whole new world to me. It's so much better than being in the closet."

Part of that involvement is being part of a team that acts as a liaison between the police and the gay community, something Rob sees as important because of the historically turbulent relationship between gay people and the police. "The pivotal event of our movement for gay and lesbian equality was Stonewall, which was essentially a confrontation between police and the gay community. So a lot of gay people do question the police and what we do, and it's good for me to talk to people who might not have a positive perception of the police. We have a team that acts as a liaison between the department and the community. We maintain a voice-mail line so that if people from the gay community have questions about how the police do something or have an issue where they really want to talk to a gay or lesbian officer, they can call that number and be assured that whoever calls them back will be a gay or lesbian officer."

Something else Rob enjoys is speaking to young people. "I never thought I couldn't be a police officer because I was gay," he says. "But I know a lot of young people do think that. One of the things our liaison team does is meet with gay and lesbian youth. We have the opportunity to meet and speak with them on a fairly regular basis, and it continually astounds me how police work doesn't seem like an option to them. That's exactly the reason why gay people *should* go into police work. I think a lot of the problems that are facing police departments today—perceptions of racism, homophobia, etc.—is because a lot of people think the police department is made up of a bunch of racists and homophobes. So because of that, a lot of the people who should be thinking about becoming police officers aren't thinking about it.

"We need more people to come out," Rob says, speaking about the absence of role models for gay young people. "Someone once said something that really spoke to me. He said that, in a sense, gay kids are orphans. Black kids have black parents. Hispanic kids have hispanic parents. But gay and lesbian kids typically have straight parents. So where do they get their sense of who they are and where they fit in? That really sums up why we need to have more people come out so that young people have people to see and to maybe look up to."

And it's not just young people that Rob's being out affects. He also challenges the beliefs of the people in his community who might not understand what being gay is all about. "Seeing gay police officers really makes people think," he says. "It's like, they'll allow you to pull them out of a burning car or grab the bad guys when they're break-ing into their houses, but they don't want to give us the same rights they have because we're gay. This makes them question those attitudes."

CELEBRATING BEING GAY

For many gay people, the hardest part of accepting ourselves isn't realizing that we are gay, or even coming to believe that being gay is not the awful thing people may tell us it is. For most of us the hardest thing is figuring out what to do on a day-to-day basis to maintain our newfound pride, stability, or sense of peace once we've come out and begun to explore the gay community. After the initial intense feelings we experience when we acknowledge our gayness, whether those are feelings of relief, fear, or joy, we then have to settle in to living our everyday lives.

This can be very difficult. Often when we are discovering who and what we are, we get very excited and enthused about ourselves and become filled with a desire and determination to be proud and to go out and conquer the world. Then, as the days go on, we realize that not every day is going to be wonderful and exciting and that sometimes it's really hard to be excited about being gay. When that happens, it's easy to get depressed or discouraged. We can feel like it's too hard or that we won't make it through another day of dealing with family, friends, jobs, and everything else in our lives.

The good news is that this happens to everyone and that it's perfectly normal. Getting discouraged doesn't mean that you're not doing something right or that there's something wrong with you. It means you're just like the rest of us. The other good news is that there are a lot of ways to deal with feeling down and to help establish a sense of peace and a positive attitude.

The most important thing to remember is that this is an ongoing process. Accepting yourself isn't something you do once and then forget about, and developing a positive attitude doesn't come from any one thing. These are things you have to do every day of your life, no matter how old you are or where you are in life. This self-acceptance, and a positive attitude, is important for everyone, not just gay people, but we have a little more work to do than most people because we face different daily struggles because of our gayness.

Developing a positive attitude involves being with other gay people, those with whom you can discuss your feelings and your concerns, people with whom you can feel relaxed enough to be yourself. Being isolated from other gay people puts a terrible strain on us because, whether we realize it or not, it makes us feel alone and reinforces negative ideas about being gay.

Part of being a member of the gay community means being with other gay people. If at all possible, try to find something you can do with other gay people, whether it's singing in a gay chorus or helping stuff envelopes at a community center. If you live in an area with a small gay community, organize a group of women and men who get together for dinners or do other activities together like going to movies, camping, or playing softball. This interaction with other gay women and men achieves many things, including making the community stronger, providing you with potential new friends or possibly even partners, and making you feel like part of your community.

This doesn't mean you have to spend all of your time with other gay people or doing gay things. There are times when I don't even want to see another gay person or think about gay issues or do anything even remotely gay. We all get "gayed out" sometimes. But there are other times when it can really help to have that gay connection, to be immersed in something that reminds us of all the positive things there are about being gay.

One good way to maintain a sense of identity and pride is to treat yourself to what I call gay dates. These are simply times you take to enjoy gay things, whether it's music, books, artwork, television programs, art exhibits, or movies. These are times when you get to be gay with nobody to answer to except yourself. You get to do anything you want to do and be whoever you want to be without having to worry what people will think or say.

Pick a time when you can be relaxed and, if not totally alone, then at least private. Your time can be an entire day, an afternoon or evening, or even just an hour during the week. Try and choose a time when work is done and you don't have to be anywhere. What's important is that it be your special time to be with yourself. You don't want to have any interruptions or worries.

83

Your gay date can be anything you want it to be. Do things that make you feel good as a gay person. It could be something as simple as taking a long bath and reading a Dorothy Allison novel, Paul Monette's biography, or a book of poems by Audre Lorde. Or maybe you want to do something more elaborate, like lighting some candles, playing some music by musicians like the Indigo Girls or Ferron, and writing in your journal about what's going on in your life or writing your own stories, poems, or songs. You might want to rent movies like *Salmonberries, Longtime Companion, Maurice,* or *Boys on the Side* and watch them. If you live in a city with a large gay population, maybe you'd like to go see a gay photo exhibit or go to some kind of gay theater presentation.

You can even have gay dates where all you do is take yourself out. One of my favorite things to do is to go to movies by myself. It's very relaxing sitting in the dark theater with no ringing phone, nothing that has to be done, and no one to bother me. A friend of mine who also likes to do gay dates enjoys packing herself a lunch and going into the woods or to the seashore. She finds a quiet place and just sits there enjoying being by herself or maybe reading.

Sometimes just being alone and quiet can make you feel refreshed and calm. If you are in a city, you can go to a museum, a park, or even an aquarium and spend an afternoon by yourself free from pressure. If you live in the country, you can walk in the woods, sit by a stream, ride your bike or horse down a new path, or float on an inner tube all alone in a pond.

The possibilities for gay dates are almost endless. You can do anything that makes you happy. The point of them is to give you a time all of your own when you can be happy about being gay and when you can read, listen to, or watch things created by other lesbian and gay people. By doing these things, you are reminding yourself of all the good things there are about being gay. Sometimes it's hard to remember that there is *anything* good about it, especially when people are giving us a hard time or we're feeling depressed. But there are good things, and reminding ourselves of that can help us make it through tough days or make a good day even better.

These things may seem silly to you. You might think the idea of taking yourself on a date, especially one where you celebrate being lesbian or gay, is ridiculous. But try one. Even if it's just allowing yourself to sit and listen to one CD you really like, write one poem about your life, or read one chapter in a book. By giving yourself time to express yourself as a gay person or to enjoy things that other gay people have done, you are helping to create a positive self-image for yourself. You are telling yourself that you are worth caring about, and that being gay is something worth celebrating.

If you are a person who has to keep your gayness a secret for whatever reason, then gay dates are a wonderful way for you to be yourself without having to tell anyone. You can always buy a book or borrow it from the library, and you can always buy a CD of music that you like. And you can certainly always write a poem or story. Even if you just take a hot bath and think about how wonderful your life can be, that's doing something important for yourself. Taking yourself on a gay date is a way of letting yourself be free, even if it's just for half an hour.

There are also many more public opportunities to celebrate being gay. One good way is by attending one of the many gay pride celebrations held in various cities around the country each June. New York, San Francisco, and Boston all have big pride celebrations, and many other cities also have their own annual parties for the gay community. These celebrations are times when gay people come together to simply enjoy being gay by having parties, dances, parades, concerts, theater performances, and many other things.

Another big occasion for gay and lesbian people is National Coming Out Day. Held each year on October 11, it is a day when gay people are encouraged to come out to one person they have never told about themselves. This can mean telling family members or friends, or it can mean wearing a National Coming Out Day pin or T-shirt to work. The idea is to celebrate being out-and-proud gay people by letting others know about ourselves. It can be an amazing experience to actually sit someone down or call someone up and tell her that you're gay, even if that person already knows but you've just never discussed it openly.

These kinds of celebrations are important because they remind us that being gay is lots of fun. Yes, the gay pride celebrations also have their serious sides, and are meant to remind us of what still needs to be done. But primarily they are times for letting loose and just having a great time with other gay people.

Other ways to celebrate being gay include going to gay art exhibits, theater performances, concerts, dances, lectures, and readings. All of these things are opportunities for you as a gay person to see or hear what other gay people have created and to find out what other men and women have experienced as gay people. Not only can this be just plain fun, it helps to remind us of the many talented people in our community.

Celebrating being gay, however, doesn't mean running around every second of your life waving a rainbow flag or wearing pink triangles on everything you own. What it means is reminding yourself about the positive things about being gay. So keep in mind that whatever you do to celebrate being part of the gay community, all of them are worthwhile.

12

GAY AND LESBIAN MOVIES AVAILABLE ON VIDEO

1. *Parting Glances*
2. *The Incredibly True Adventures of Two Girls in Love*
3. *Jeffrey*
4. *Go Fish*
5. *Longtime Companion*
6. *Desert Hearts*
7. *Torch Song Trilogy*
8. *Personal Best*
9. *My Beautiful Laundrette*
10. *Bar Girls*
11. *To Wong Foo, Thanks for Everything, Julie Newmar*
10. *The Adventures of Priscilla, Queen of the Desert*

A NOTE TO GAY YOUNG PEOPLE

Growing up, many of us receive positive messages about ourselves or our achievements from friends, parents, teachers, coaches, and other people in our lives. These people tell us that our poems are good, that our batting is solid, that the muffins we bake taste great, and that our piano playing is beautiful, sometimes even if none of these things are really true. These things make us feel good about ourselves and give us a sense of self-worth. The positive messages make us feel that what we do is important, that who we are is important.

Sometimes, though, we don't have people doing these things for us. Gay young people especially can often find themselves in situations where it seems no one is paying attention or where no one is giving positive feedback about anything. Our parents react in embarrassment when we show them a poem, because they think we should be playing soccer instead. Our friends laugh when we join chorus instead of track. Our brothers and sisters ask us not to tell anyone that we take ballet or like to go camping because it "ruins their reputations." These things can be very hard on us, because it sends out the message that what we are doing is not good enough, that somehow we aren't worthy enough to deserve attention or praise.

Even those of us who do get positive attention from people may feel less positive when it comes to being gay. Being the captain of the baseball team or the soloist in the choir doesn't make it any easier for you if you still feel bad about being a gay person. It's one thing to say that we should all have pride in ourselves. It's another thing to be proud of being different when someone at school teases you for liking classical music or for wearing clothes that you like, or when someone starts gossip about your being gay. When those things happen, it's very easy to feel bad and to feel ashamed of being gay.

So what do you do when these things happen? You live through them. You tell yourself that the people teasing you or giving you a hard time don't know anything about you, and that what they say doesn't matter. Then you go home and you cry, work out, play the clarinet loudly, turn up your favorite record as high as possible, go running or swimming until you're exhausted, or whatever it is you need to do to work out your anger and frustration. When you've done that, then you take time to do something you enjoy, like reading a favorite book, listening to a favorite album, throwing pitches, sitting on a favorite rock or in a favorite tree, or writing a poem or story. You do something that makes you feel good about yourself.

What you shouldn't do is replay the event over and over in your head. Don't dwell on what was said or what someone did. Use the time of intense running, playing, singing, or whatever you choose to express your anger and frustration. During that time, think about the situation as much as you want to. Let anything you feel come and go. When you feel yourself getting mad again, play louder or run faster. When you feel as though you've thought about it enough, or when you've worked out your anger by running, playing the piano, or whatever, let it go. It isn't worth your time to keep thinking about it.

The other thing you should not to do is stop doing things you enjoy because people might tease you. That will only make you feel worse, and you won't even have the enjoyment you were getting out of the activity. If someone teases you for writing poetry, not writing poetry anymore isn't going to make you feel better. It might stop the teasing, and that might feel good for a while, but you will always feel that writing poetry is somehow bad, and you will be proving the person teasing you right by letting her teasing make you give up something you really enjoy. Or if you stop playing softball because someone says it's not right for you to play, you hurt yourself just because some ignorant person told you that what you love to do is wrong.

If other people are not going to make us feel good about ourselves, then it's up to us to make ourselves feel good. No, it isn't fair. We all deserve to be told that we are worthwhile. But for a lot of different reasons, sometimes that doesn't happen. We can't depend on other people to make us happy, or to make us feel good about ourselves. While what people say to us or do to us can affect how we feel about ourselves, ultimately happiness and a positive attitude come from knowing inside that we *are* worthwhile.

One way to develop and keep a positive attitude is simply to accept the fact that every one of us deserves the chance to be happy. No matter what people tell you—your parents, your friends, your priests or rabbis or ministers, your teachers, people at school or work, your coaches—you are someone who deserves to be treated well. It doesn't matter what your grades are, what sports you can play, what activities you are involved in, what you're good at, or what job you have. The person you are right now is a person who deserves respect.

That is a very hard thing for most of us to believe. We are often determined to be unhappy, or to believe that we don't deserve anything good. Odd as it may sound, a lot of times it's easier to be unhappy than it is to be happy. Being miserable is a snap—all we have to do is decide that everything always goes wrong and that everything bad that happens is something we deserve. Being happy is harder. It's something you have to learn how to do, and something you have to practice.

Once you've accepted that you are someone who has the right to feel good, remind yourself of this every day. If people tell you there's something wrong with the way you act, dress, or look, remember that what they're reacting to is what they think people should be like. No one set up any rules about how people have to be, and even if they did, you wouldn't have to follow them. You are who you are, and maybe that person isn't like everyone else. Maybe that person will frighten other people because they wish they had the courage to be who they are. We are often taught to believe that the easiest way to be happy is to fit in and be like everyone else. Well, maybe it's easier to do that than to put up with what people say or do when we're different, but it kills a little bit of us every time we give in to what people want us to be.

Another thing that can help you maintain a positive attitude is to remind yourself of things you've done that you are proud of. It doesn't matter if anyone else knows about them or not. What matters is that you are happy about them.

As gay people, one of the main reasons we feel unhappy is because we feel trapped—by school and work, by where we live, and often by our families. Often we can feel as if we'll never get out, never be away from all of these pressures. We feel we can't be ourselves, can't do things we'd really like to do, and maybe can't even buy the books, magazines, or records we'd like to because we live at home. Every day seems like an obstacle course we have to run through with people trying to stop us at every turn.

If living day to day is hard for you because you feel stuck in some place you hate, or you are in a situation that makes you sad, remind yourself that it won't be forever. If you're in school and hate it, think about what you want to do after you graduate. Make plans for your new life, even if they don't seem realistic. Allow yourself to dream about what the possibilities are. This won't make the difficult situations go away, but it will make you realize that nothing is forever.

Whatever you do, don't beat yourself up when you feel bad. Allow yourself to think of all the good things about you and about your life, no matter how small they are. Every one of us has bad days or even weeks. Some of us even have bad months and years. They're always going to come and go. But we can help ourselves through them by reminding ourselves that, whatever happens to us, there's always something good waiting to happen. It might take longer than we like, but it will happen if we let it. And if bad things happen to us, it isn't because we're gay or because we're bad people; it's because sometimes there are things we need to go through to make us stronger. Knowing and believing that we're already strong enough is what helps us keep going.

10

GREAT BOOKS FOR GAY YOUNG PEOPLE

1. **ANNIE ON MY MIND,** Nancy Garden

2. **AM I BLUE?,** edited by Marion Dane Bauer

3. **THE WEETZIE BAT SERIES,** Francesca Lia Block

4. **I HADN'T MEANT TO TELL YOU THIS,** Jacqueline Woodson

5. **JACK,** A. M. Homes

6. **THE CAT CAME BACK,** Hillary Mullins

7. **THE MAN WITHOUT A FACE,** Isabelle Holland

8. **NIGHT KITES,** M.E. Kerr

9. **CRUSH,** Jane Futcher

10. **UNLIVED AFFECTIONS,** George Shannon

SEATTLE, WASHINGTON — Karen Taylor

Situated on the water and surrounded by the mountains and beautiful redwood forests of the Pacific Northwest, Seattle is one of the most beautiful cities in the United States. It is also becoming an increasingly popular city for gay people to live in, and the city's gay community is growing larger every year. Unlike other cities popular with gay people, like New York or Chicago, Seattle is much more laid back and relaxed. Yet it still offers many of the exciting things that larger cities do.

While Seattle is a city, it really feels more like a big town with extra neighbors. The city is home to many different groups of people, which makes the population diverse and interesting. It is a city of neighborhoods, and each has its own personality. For instance, Belltown is the home of the alternative arts scene, and is very gay-friendly. Pioneer Square is the oldest part of the city, and home to many of the homeless shelters. Ballard is like stepping into an old Norwegian fishing town. The International District and Beacon Hill are heavily Asian American, while the African-American neighborhood is the Central District. The University District is a great place to meet students and young people. And, of course, there's the "gay" neighborhood, Capitol Hill.

The main street through Capitol Hill is Broadway, and it is a good place to shop, eat, go to the movies, grab a cup of coffee, and generally hang out in a gay atmosphere. The whole area has the feeling of being a place where gay and lesbian people can relax and be themselves with other gay people. For evening safety, the neighborhood is patroled by Queer Patrol, which works closely with the Seattle Police Department to prevent gay-bashing and harassment of gay people.

Seattle's gay community is as varied as its population and offers a lot of great opportunities for young gay people. If you're interested in finding out about what's going on, you can start by calling the twenty-four-hour gay/lesbian youth information phone line at (206)

322-7900. The line includes information on places to get food or shelter, hotlines, information on books and bookstores, social groups and/or pen pals, churches, upcoming community events, information on STDs and HIV and AIDS, general information on sexuality, and special topics of interest to gay people.

If you're looking for places to go where young adults hang out, at the top of the list is Lambert House, Seattle's drop-in center for youth who are gay, lesbian, bisexual, transgendered, or just questioning their sexuality. For women, the Lesbian Resource Center also offers information, support groups, and social activities on an on-going basis. Both of these places offer a friendly, relaxed atmosphere where people looking to find out more about Seattle's gay community can get information. They are also great places to meet other young people and make friends.

Seattle is also home to several colleges and universities, including the University of Washington, Seattle University, Seattle Community College, and a branch of Antioch University. All of the colleges, including the community college, have active gay and lesbian student groups, which are great places to start if you're looking for ways to meet other gay people. Seattle has a lot of young people, and there are many opportunities for gay young people who want to become actively involved in the city's gay community. All it takes is finding one group and exploring what's available.

To find out what's happening in Seattle's gay community, check out the local publications, starting with the *Seattle Gay News*, which contains news of interest to gay people, as well as community events. *The Stranger* is an alternative weekly with a gay bent (the advice columnist, Dan Savage, requests letters be directed to "Hey, Faggot"). The *Seattle Weekly* offers arts and cultural information, and includes a gay section in its calendar. For general information, pick up the Greater Seattle Business Association (GSBA) directory. The GSBA directory lists businesses and social groups in the lesbian and gay community. All of these publications are free.

Seattle is a very arts-oriented city, and there are a number of arts and cultural groups that provide creative outlets for gay artists, including the country's second-oldest lesbian and gay theater company, the Alice B. Theatre (named after writer Gertrude Stein's lover, Alice B. Toklas), and the nationally renowned Seattle Men's Chorus. Of course, Seattle is also known for its thriving alternative music scene, and music is a big part of the arts community. Other groups also offer entertainment on a more casual basis. Seattle's drag and leather communities have a pageant, contest, or fund-raising event nearly every weekend in one of the Capitol Hill bars. The hottest nondrinking party in town, though, is gay bingo. No fooling! As the motto says, it's just like normal bingo, only way more fun.

For clubbing, Seattle's scene is large and diverse. Unlike many cities, in Seattle gays and straights mix pretty freely, and a lot of places are frequented by both gay and non-gay crowds without any trouble. In fact, many of Seattle's non-gay clubs post notices warning customers that they will not tolerate homophobic, racist, or sexist comments, and you'll find straight and gay folk dancing and hanging out together in clubs in Belltown and the University District, as well as in Capitol Hill. There are also a lot of bars and clubs just for gay people.

Seattle's lesbian and gay community is heavily active in local politics. In addition to working on various campaigns and getting involved with the local political parties, the city has a Commission for Lesbians and Gays that acts as an adviser to the mayor. In 1992, the first African-American lesbian elected to office in the country was elected to the Seattle City Council. The political climate in Seattle is very positive in terms of supporting all kinds of human rights, and this includes gay rights.

Because of its location, Seattle is also home to innumerable recreational opportunities, including hiking, skiing, swimming, running, and biking, and the gay community takes part in all of them enthusiastically. Just grab a GSBA directory and look under "sports." You're sure to find at least one club organized around your favorite activity. These clubs are great ways to meet other gay people and enjoy something you love to do at the same time.

People move from all over the country to live in Seattle because of its beauty, its livability, and its many educational and work opportunities. For lesbians and gays, Seattle offers a lot of interesting and fun ways to meet other gay people in an atmosphere of tolerance. While homophobia exists here, as it does everywhere, Seattle does something about it. The city is not only more tolerant of lesbians and gays, it is also intolerant of homophobia. The rights of gay people are protected here. That can make a lot of difference when you're looking for a place to visit—or to call home.

KAREN TAYLOR has lived in Seattle for ten years, and has been active in the lesbian/gay community for most of that time. She served for seven years on the board of Alice B. Theatre, and has served on several other boards of community organizations. She moved to Seattle on a whim, never having been west of the Mississippi River before, and has stayed ever since.

COMMUNITY HISTORY AND ROLE MODELS

Growing up, we often have other people held up to us as role models for what we should be like or what we should do with our lives. Sports figures, actors, writers, activists, and, less often, politicians are all presented as people we should admire and want to be like. Relatives and parents frequently ask us what we want to be and whom we admire. Our answers to these questions bring either approval or disapproval, depending on our choices.

For most people, there are many role models to choose from, women and men who represent the most successful, happy, and accomplished people from a particular community. From a young age, we see pictures of these people in classrooms, read about them in books and magazines, and hear their accomplishments discussed in conversations. As we grow older, we may even decide that we want to be like one or more of these people we've heard so much about.

Gay people are not brought up to have heroes or role models. As children, no one ever points out lesbian and gay people and tells us how great they are or asks us if we want to be like them when we grow up. We don't see gay people celebrated in books or on television. Our teachers don't put up pictures of gay people and ask us to write reports about them. We don't learn about gay people or gay culture in our history classes. We aren't told about all of the wonderful things gay people have contributed to society over the years.

The result of this invisibility is that most of us grow up thinking that no gay person ever did anything worthwhile, and that everyone who accomplishes anything in life must be straight. The message is that probably we won't accomplish anything, either, because somehow we are different in a way that makes us not as important as these people being held up as heroes. Because we don't read about, see, or hear about gay people, we don't realize that all around us gay people are contributing great things to the worlds of science, sports, medicine, art, politics, and many other areas. Because we don't read in history books that many famous people were gay, we end up with the weird perception that being gay was something invented in the 1970s in San Francisco along with disco and really bad clothes. We are never taught the rich and exciting history of our community.

The fact is that gay and lesbian people have been contributing to society throughout history, whether we know who they are or not and whether or not other people want to admit it. But because being gay was not something people often talked about or were able to be open about, we will probably never know exactly how many women and men from our community contributed great things to the world. Many well-known people were gay, but this fact has been neatly left out of official biographies because it might be embarrassing to someone or because someone didn't want people to know that a gay person actually achieved something. Even when we do know of someone being gay, that fact won't be discussed in history books. Many of us read the works of Walt Whitman, one of America's greatest poets, in high school English classes. But how many English books mention that the author of *Leaves of Grass* was gay? How many history texts discuss the homosexuality of geniuses like Leonardo Da Vinci, or mention that there is strong evidence that America's most beloved First Lady, Eleanor Roosevelt, had a long lesbian relationship?

Gay and lesbian people have effectively been written out of history. Some people will argue that this is because a person's sexuality really isn't as important as what she or he accomplished, and that it doesn't matter if someone was gay or not. This is partially true. But at the same time, for those of us who searched desperately for any signs of the existence of gay people, it would have been reassuring to know that some of our favorite artists were gay, that some of our most brilliant writers were lesbians, or that some of the greatest discoveries in science, archaeology, and exploration were made by gay women and men.

Hiding the sexualities of well-known people is common practice, even today. How many times have we heard rumors about a favorite star being gay, only to have that person suddenly get married or spend lots of time vehemently denying the stories? Often a person's sexuality is an open secret in the gay community, but not to the world at large. In effect, the person is still invisible as a role model to people who would benefit hugely from knowing that someone gay was in Congress or led a mission into space. Imagine how many young people, struggling with accepting themselves, would benefit from knowing that the famous actress who also directed their favorite movie was a lesbian, or that the quarterback who led his team to the Superbowl victory was gay.

In recent years some famous people have started to come out of the closet, including tennis great Martina Navratilova, actress and director Amanda Bearse of *Married...with Children,* actor Sir Ian McKellan, actor and writer Dan Butler of *Frasier,* and singers k.d. lang, Melissa Etheridge, Melissa Ferrick, and Boy George. The list of out women and men continues to grow, particularly in the fields of music and the arts. For many people, especially young people, these women and men represent something very special. They are reminders that, far from being the awful people we are sometimes told we are, gay people are some of the most talented people in the world. We can be anything we want to be, and we can do what we want to do without having to hide who we are. We can be gay and successful, gay and talented, gay and happy.

On an everyday level, there are gay women and men in every part of society. Because we usually look and act like everyone else, it's not always easy to see the gay people around us, so people looking for gay role models might not always find them. But they're there fighting fires, teaching English, coaching baseball teams, arguing in courts, running businesses, making movies, raising children, leading churches and synagogues, plowing fields, and climbing mountains. Often these men and women come out publicly, providing gay people with more and more role models. Hopefully, the next generation of gay people will have hundreds and hundreds of women and men to look up to.

In the same way that we have been denied gay role models, we have also been denied gay history. Few history classes discuss the fact that gay women and men were actively hunted down and killed during the Holocaust, or that throughout history gay people have been routinely subjected to persecution. Many gay people know nothing about early gay rights groups; the Mattachine Society, the Gay Liberation Front, and Daughters of Bilitis were some of the first gay community groups in this country.

Most gay people know something about the 1969 Stonewall Riots, which effectively launched the modern gay rights movement. But before Stonewall there were decades during which gay women and men had to hide their sexuality for fear of being imprisoned, hospitalized as mentally ill, and abused by their families and society. Few young people today read about the underground gay groups that for many years were the only support for gay women and men in this country, or about the thousands of lesbians who spent their lives posing as men in order to get jobs and live in straight society in the 1940s, '50s, and '60s. This is our history as gay people, and it is a very important history. But we are not taught this history because it has been excised out of the "official" history of America.

10 NOTABLE LESBIAN AND BISEXUAL WOMEN FROM PAST HISTORY

1. **SAPPHO:** Ancient Greek
2. **GERTRUDE STEIN:** Writer
3. **MAY SARTON:** Writer
4. **VIRGINIA WOOLF:** Writer and activist
5. **WILLA CATHER:** Writer
6. **SUSAN B. ANTHONY:** Activist
7. **MARLENE DIETRICH:** Actress
8. **ELEANOR ROOSEVELT:** Activist and author
9. **KAY THOMPSON:** Actress and children's book author
10. **EDITH HEAD:** Costume designer

As gay people, it is important that we resurrect this history. Much as African Americans and Native Americans have reclaimed figures from those cultures and made learning about the history of those cultures something to be cherished, we need to make learning about gay history and gay figures a part of who we are. Finding out about the history of the gay community, and about the women and men who make up our community, can give us a sense of pride in being gay and in being part of a vibrant family. When we realize what the gay community has accomplished, it can help us see the enormous gains we have made and the possibilities available to us.

Reclaiming gay history takes many forms. First and foremost, it means learning more about who we are, both as individuals and as a community. There are many interesting books available that detail the history of the gay community and the lives of the women and men who have made up the community and who continue to be part of it. A selection of some of these books is listed at the end of this chapter. Reading these books may give you a better sense of what the gay community has endured.

Reclaiming history also means collecting our history. There are several groups dedicated to gay history. The Lesbian Herstory Archives in Brooklyn, New York, contains enormous amounts of information about the history of lesbian life in the United States. Also in New York, the Lesbian and Gay Community Services Center is home to an extensive archive of gay materials, from photographs and diaries to letters and newspaper articles. These places are wonderful because they bring together many different

10 NOTABLE GAY AND BISEXUAL MEN FROM PAST HISTORY

1. **ROCK HUDSON:** Actor

2. **JAMES BALDWIN:** Writer and civil rights activist

3. **GEORGE CUKOR:** Film director

4. **LEONARDO DA VINCI:** Renaissance artist and inventor

5. **PETER TCHAIKOVSKY:** Composer

6. **ALAN TURING:** Mathematician

7. **COLE PORTER:** Composer

8. **TENNESSEE WILLIAMS:** Playwright

9. **NOEL COWARD:** Playwright, actor, composer

10. **ANDRÉ GIDE:** Writer

aspects of gay life and preserve them. As long as these reminders of our history are kept safe, we can never again be written out of history.

As gay people, it is important for us to know about our history because it reminds us of what we have achieved and what we have yet to achieve, and because it reminds us that despite all we are taught to believe, gay women and men have been contributing significantly to the world for centuries and are continuing to do so. Knowing this gives us a sense of pride and reminds us that we are part of an extraordinary group of people.

There are many different kinds of books about gay and lesbian history and culture. The ones listed below are considered some of the best and are great places to start exploring. Some are serious histories, others are collections of personal essays written by people from the community. All of them reflect a different aspect of gay and lesbian life.

BÉRUBÉ, ALLAN, *Coming Out Under Fire: The History of Gay Men and Lesbians in World War Two* (New York: Plume, 1991).

CRUIKSHANK, MARGARET, *The Gay and Lesbian Liberation Movement* (New York: Routledge, 1992).

DUBERMAN, MARTIN, *About Time: Exploring the Gay Past* (New York: Meridian, 1991).

DUBERMAN, MARTIN, *Stonewall* (New York: Dutton, 1993).

DUBERMAN, MARTIN, MARTHA VICINUS, AND GEORGE CHAUNCEY, JR., eds., *Hidden from History: Reclaiming the Gay and Lesbian Past* (New York: Meridian, 1989).

FADERMAN, LILLIAN, *Odd Girls and Twilight Lovers: A History of Lesbian Life in Twentieth-Century America* (New York: Penguin, 1991).

KATZ, JONATHAN NED, *Gay American History: Lesbians and Gay Men in the USA* (New York: Meridian, 1992).

LANE, MICHAEL, *Pink Highways: Tales of Queer Madness on the Open Road* (New York: Birch Lane Press, 1995).

LUCZAK, RAYMOND, *Eyes of Desire: A Deaf Gay and Lesbian Reader* (Boston: Alyson Publications, 1993).

MARCUS, ERIC, *Making History: The Struggle for Gay and Lesbian Equal Rights 1945-1990* (New York: HarperCollins, 1992).

MILLER, NEIL, *Out of the Past: Gay and Lesbian History from 1869 to the Present* (New York: Vintage, 1995).

PLANT, RICHARD, *The Pink Triangle: The Nazi War Against Homosexuals* (New York: Henry Holt, 1986).

PRICE, DEB AND JOYCE MURDOCH, *And Say Hi to Joyce for Me: America's First Gay Column Comes Out* (New York: Doubleday, 1995).

ROGERS, SUSAN FOX, *Sportsdykes: Stories from On and Off the Field* (New York: St. Martin's Press, 1994).

DATING AND RELATIONSHIPS

One area that most gay people have questions and concerns about is dating and having relationships. There are the pressures of asking someone to go out or to get married. There are the pressures of wondering if so-and-so finds us attractive. I imagine that most people would say that dating is one of the hardest, most stressful part of their lives. This can be especially difficult for young people.

Well, straight people have a walk in the park compared to what gay people go through. Not only do we have to worry about whether he thinks we're cute or if she wants to go out, we have to worry about whether someone is even gay! Before we worry about where to go on that first date or whether or not to kiss her goodnight, we have to know if she's a lesbian. It seems like getting from that first, "I think he's really cute and wouldn't it be great to date him" feeling to actually doing it is like running through an obstacle course blindfolded with your arms tied behind your back.

We don't really think about it much, but in many ways straight people really are taught how to date and form relationships. People grow up surrounded by images of women and men going on dates, worrying about being asked to the prom, talking to boyfriends and girlfriends on the phone, getting married, and even talking about their relationships with friends and family members. By the time straight people are old enough to date, they've already seen how it works or had the experiences of their friends and siblings to follow. In fact, straight people are expected to start dating when they reach a certain age. It's all a part of growing up in our society.

As gay people we don't have any of those things. Television shows don't depict young lesbians worrying about whom to ask to the prom. We don't see images of gay men sitting around with their friends talking about which guys at work are really cute. Most of us don't have older gay siblings we can talk to about boy problems and girl problems. Even magazines for young people are all about heterosexual lives. You don't see teen magazines talking about gay or lesbian people and their dating issues or about ten sure ways to get that cute dyke in your sociology class to notice you. And few parents wait for the day when their daughter takes the most beautiful girl in school out on her first date or their son announces that the school quarterback has asked him to the movies.

Not having these images means that as gay people we really have no basis for reflecting on what relationships should be. Since we don't see ads that show two women going to a concert on a first date or read articles about living with the same man for fifteen years, it's almost as if gay relationships don't exist. This can make it very hard for us as gay people to picture ourselves dating in the same way that our straight friends date.

To make things even harder, when we do go on dates as gay people, or go out with our lovers, we often can't express ourselves the way two straight people can. In most places, it's hard for two young women to hold hands while they walk through the park or for two young men to have a romantic dinner at a restaurant without attracting negative attention or comments from other people. The fears we have over possibly being harassed make a dating situation even harder, and acting as though we're just good friends with the person we are with can make us feel bad or make us feel that somehow we aren't on a "real" date or in a "real" relationship.

This can make us feel as if we don't get to have the same kind of dating experiences that straight people do. And in many ways we don't. For one thing, straight people pretty much have everyone of the opposite sex to choose from for potential dates. While a straight guy can't necessarily *get* a date with every girl he's interested in, at least he knows he can *ask* a girl out. But a gay man or woman doesn't have that option. We have to work even harder just to find people to ask out in the first place. We also have to look for people who are comfortable enough with themselves as lesbian or gay people that they are even ready to date someone else.

All of this is a lot to ask. For these reasons, a lot of gay people never experience dating in a positive way and never learn how to form successful relationships. As odd as this may seem, what it means is that when we come out and are able to meet other gay people, we don't really know how to go about dating them. It's as if we have to learn all of the things straight people learn about dating when we're much older. We may be twenty-five years old and going on our first real date with someone. This sounds funny, but to people who feel that they missed out on a whole part of growing up, it can be very hard to handle. It can also make it much harder to meet people in a relaxed way.

Today, a lot of gay young people do date and have relationships. In many ways, these young people are breaking new ground. Having your boyfriend over for dinner with your parents isn't something most gay men would ever have thought about when they were growing up. Taking your girlfriend to the movies or out dancing isn't something a lot of lesbians did in high school or even college. And there are certainly a lot of gay young people who date without their parents knowing about it.

If you are dating, you have a wonderful opportunity to learn a lot about yourself and what you want out of life and out of a relationship. Dating should be a time when you learn how to get to know someone and how to communicate with someone. While asking people out and dealing with our expectations and anxieties can make us very nervous, dating should be a relaxing time to enjoy being with someone else.

What dating shouldn't be is harmful. This is true whether we're straight or gay. We should never date someone who abuses us in any way. An obvious example of this is someone who hits you. You should never, for any reason, remain in a relationship with someone who slaps or hits you. Anyone who does that doesn't respect you, and you shouldn't waste your time being with her or him.

But abuse can be other things as well, things we often don't recognize as being abuse until much later. Someone telling you that you aren't going to be happy without him or without her is abusing you. Someone telling you that no one else will ever like you or love you is abusing you. Anything someone says or does to put you down or to make you feel bad about yourself is abuse. Even someone telling you that your dreams and hopes are silly or unrealistic is a form of abuse, because it makes you feel less important than you are.

Many people complain about not having lovers. They think that life would be great if they just found that special someone. But because they are in such a hurry, they will often date people who just aren't right for them. They overlook the bad things and pretend the good things are better than they really are. They believe that having any kind of girlfriend or boyfriend is better than being alone, so they put up with people who don't really care about them or whose behavior isn't what it should be.

Probably the most important thing to remember about relationships is that you don't need to have one to be a happy person. Too often people say, "If only I had a boyfriend everything would be fine" or "If I just had a girlfriend I wouldn't be so depressed." Having a boyfriend or girlfriend can be an amazing experience, but it won't change who you are. It may change how you feel about some things, and it may make you happier, but don't look for a relationship to change everything about your life.

A relationship should be something that enhances your life, not something you look for to make everything in your life better. As romantic as it sounds, finding the perfect woman or man isn't going to make all of your problems suddenly go away. You're going to be the same person with the same struggles you had before you had a lover. It's just that with a boyfriend or girlfriend to worry about, you have some new and different struggles to deal with.

Don't be in such a hurry to find a girlfriend or a boyfriend that you make the mistake of getting attached to the first person who comes along. Believe it or not, you are going to have lots of opportunities to date different kinds of people. You don't have to date someone just because she or he seems to be the only thing around. And if someone isn't treating you the right way, or really is making you unhappy, you don't have to stay with her or with him just because being alone seems depressing. No matter how attractive someone is, or how much money she has, or how much anything, being in a relationship with someone who isn't right for you is going to be harder and more painful than saying good-bye is going to be.

A special word is needed here about relationships between young people and older people. Sometimes gay young people do find themselves involved with people several years older than themselves. While often these relationships can be positive ones, you should be aware that in some states it is illegal for adults to have sex with people under a certain age, usually eighteen, which is considered the age when you become an adult. This isn't to say that everyone who is in a relationship is necessarily having sex. Many people aren't. But you should be aware that the older person in the relationship could face legal problems if someone decided to make an issue out of it and say that the two of you are having sex.

Another issue you may face if you are involved with someone older than yourself is that she or he tries to control your life. The person may tell you what to do, always demand to know where you are, pressure you to do things you don't want to do or do other things that make you feel unhappy. This can also happen with someone your own age, but it is more likely to happen with someone who wants to think he or she knows more than you do or with someone who wants to "take care of you." Because you are younger, you might find it difficult to say no to the older person or to say what you really feel. You might be afraid of losing the person, making him or her angry, or of appearing to be immature. But it is important for you to remember that you are in control of your own life. If you find that someone you are involved with tries to control what you do or who you are, you have to get out of that relationship.

Every one of us has a different experience when it comes to dating and relationships. I didn't have my first boyfriend until I was twenty-one. Other people I know had girlfriends and boyfriends when they were in high school or college. It all depends on what kind of person you are, where you live, and what kind of support there is for gay people. If you aren't dating yet, you have a lot to look forward to. Learning all about someone else can be a wonderful experience, and it will teach you many things about yourself as well. Sharing things with another person you care about is one of the most exciting things we can do in life. Just don't worry about rushing it. It will happen when you're ready.

If you have found someone whom you think is just perfect for you, then congratulations. It's a wonderful thing when you meet someone who makes you feel good and with whom you can share different parts of your life. This is especially wonderful for gay young people, since it's so much harder for us to accomplish. If you are in a positive dating situation, or even in a relationship that has been going on for quite a while, you have really achieved something, and you should be proud of yourself.

FLOOD, GREGORY, *I'm Looking for Mr. Right, But I'd Settle for Mr. Right Now* (Seattle, WA: Brob House, 1994).

MARCUS, ERIC, *The Male Couple's Guide: Finding a Man, Making a Home, Building a Life* (New York: HarperCollins, 1992).

MCDANIEL, JUDITH, *The Lesbian Couple's Guide: Finding the Right Woman and Creating a Life Together* (New York: HarperCollins, 1995).

JAMES JOHNSTONE, LAURA MAYNE, AND JAYKA MAYNE:
REDEFINING FAMILY

For many gay and lesbian people, the idea of having a family and children seems an impossibility. Because we are brought up to believe that the definition of *family* can only mean one particular thing, we think that we have to give up having family and children if we want to live as gay people. Fortunately, this is not true. More and more gay and lesbian people are forming their own kinds of families and are having and raising children of their own. Rather than be limited by the old definition of family, we are redefining what a family is.

James Johnstone and Laura Mayne are such a family. James, a gay man, and Laura, a lesbian, both wanted to have a child. Using artificial insemination, they created their daughter, Jayka Mayne. Born in October 1994, Jayka lives with her mother. James lives near by and spends a lot of time with Laura and Jayka. But their family also consists of many different people, all of whom play important roles in Jayka's life.

For James, the opportunity to have a child came at a time when he was just discovering his desire to have a child in his life. "For many years, I had never thought of being a parent or having children in my life," he says, "until my brother had a baby son. From the moment that I held that baby in my arms, I realized that I had a very strong parenting instinct. The day after the baby was born, talking with my sister-in-law on the phone and hearing this little baby squeak, something melted inside and I though, 'I don't know myself after all.' I was surprised at my reaction. Of course I was happy that they had a baby, but I think that like so many gay people I felt a bit like I was on the sidelines looking at what straight people are able to do in terms of family for the mere fact that they are heterosexual and that society approves of and supports them."

For Laura, having a child was something she had long dreamed of. "When I was growing up, it was always something I wanted," she says. "But then I got busy with school and other things. Then, after I

came out, I started working with women and children at a shelter and realized I really wanted children in my life. Being a lesbian didn't really seem like a conflict to me. I just knew that I would have to do things differently. So I started talking to other lesbian moms and asked about their experiences until I found a way to do it."

Laura contacted James through a mutual friend and asked him if he would consider being a sperm donor for her. "I wanted my baby to have a father in her life," Laura says of her decision not to use an anonymous donor. "I wanted her to know who her father was and to have contact with him." After meeting and discussing the various legal and personal issues about having a child together, James and Laura agreed to an arrangement where Laura would be the primary parent and James would be actively involved in the baby's life. They began the fertilization process, and Laura became pregnant shortly afterward.

Jayka Mayne's family is certainly not a traditional one. In addition to Laura and James, she is surrounded by the friends, lovers, and family members of both her parents. While she spends most of her time with her mother, she also spends time with James at his home, and she is also cared for by many loving people, all of whom James and Laura consider family. James believes that Jayka benefits greatly from this extended family. "What I see Laura having created around Jayka is this family of adults that goes beyond definition," he explains. "I'm a very proud father. But you get into definitions when you try to describe these situations, and the lines are definitely blurred here. It's basically a community bringing up this baby, and you just have to see her to see that she is being brought up with an incredible amount of love and support. She's very self-confident. She displays all of this rambunctious and exploratory joy and excitement about her environment that a baby being brought up with love and care should demonstrate, and it's a joy to watch her."

Laura agrees. "There are many different people in Jayka's life, and in mine," she says. "All of them love and support us, and it's been so wonderful to watch this family grow and change."

"What we have," adds James, "is an extended family of adults who are either related by blood or by love or by both to this baby. And you couldn't ask for a better family. And these are all of the supposedly horrible gays and lesbians who are out to pervert and destroy children and the family."

That issue of anti-gay people defining lesbian and gay parents and families as somehow wrong angers both Laura and James. "I look at the people who say we should not be a family or have families," James says, "and these are the same people who raise their children with beatings and with fear. It's all a pack of very horrid and sad lies that they perpetuate about gay people. I'm very proud and happy to be part of this family. It's been a wonderful gift to me to be involved with this child, my daughter, and I know that it's a beautiful thing we have here. This family unit that we have is the biggest threat to what the religious right calls 'traditional families,' because we fly in the face of everything that they consider good and right for children and the family unit. But here we have created out of love and agreement a family that is based on love and support. Every single person in our extended family has an agreement to be there for this baby. Because as gay people we grow up without the expectations of being parents, I think we tend to study more and really ask questions about what is the best thing about being parents. Obviously, when a gay or lesbian person has a child, it's a very conscious choice being made. It's not some accident that just happens. A lot of planning goes into it. Everyone involved has chosen to bring the child into the world."

"I'm proud because this is something we created because we wanted to instead of just falling into something that was expected," says Laura.

As Jayka grows up, Laura believes that being surrounded by so many different types of people will be good for her and will help her through any difficulties she might experience from being part of a nontraditional family. "I came to the conclusion that the more proud I can be about my life and about what I've created, the happier she'll

be and the easier it will be for her," she says. "This will be something that she grows up with, and it will seem natural to her. Plus she has all of this support around her."

Aside from being a wonderful joy in his own life, James says that one of the most exciting parts of having Jayka is that people who see how happy Jayka is, and how well their situation works, will learn something valuable. Gay people in particular he thinks are helped by seeing how successful their family arrangement has been. "A few years earlier," he says, "my ex-lover, who I still live with, had been told at a family Christmas party that his sister and brother-in-law had decided that it would be best for everybody if he never saw his nephew and niece again and never touched them. And this devastated him. I think things like that put gay people in a space where they start to doubt themselves around children, and even start to believe all of the lies that society has set around gay people and children. So watching my ex's connection with Jayka and the incredible healing that started happening there has been very, very positive. I think the more people see that this is possible, and see that we can create our own families, despite what anyone else says, the more we will come to value ourselves as people and the more we will realize that we don't have to give up anything just because we don't fit someone else's definition of what is right and acceptable."

FAMILY VALUES

Just as gay people seldom see positive images of gay people dating, we almost never hear about successful gay relationships or about gay families. In fact, we are conditioned to believe that gay women and men can never have long-term relationships or have "normal" families, and that the only way to have a family is to have a heterosexual marriage. Many gay young people say their greatest fear about being gay is that they will never have a lover or children, and many gay men and women get married simply because they don't want to give up having a family or children, yet they spend years being unhappy because they have to hide who they are.

As gay people we are not taught that we can form relationships with people of the same sex and have loving, fulfilling relationships. We are not taught that we can have children if we want them. We are not told about the gay women and men who have spent years and years together and grown old together. What we are usually told is that gay people only want to have sex with as many people as possible and aren't even capable of having serious relationships.

The truth is that gay people do form happy, successful relationships. We also have children. We can form families that are just as strong as traditional families. In this time of politicians and religious leaders talking about the need for a return to "traditional family values," what is being overlooked is the fact that more and more families are not traditional. That doesn't mean these families aren't as good as those made up of mom and dad and children. It just means they are different.

Lesbians and gay men form many different kinds of relationships. Some people live with the same person forever. Others stay with one person for a long time and then find that the relationship doesn't work any longer. And some people choose to date many different people. In other words, we do the same things straight people do. There's nothing mysterious about it.

The difference, perhaps, is that our relationships are not considered legal by other people. A gay couple cannot file their taxes jointly. If one partner in a relationship dies, the other partner is not always treated as the person's legal partner, even if they were together for twenty years. A gay partner does not have the same rights that a heterosexual partner would in the same situation. Most colleges do not provide housing for same-sex couples, even when they do for heterosexual unmarried couples.

There are some exceptions to this. Many companies now offer benefits to same-sex couples, and some cities do have laws giving gay people certain rights in regards to owning property. Some cities, like San Francisco and New York, also allow gay people to register as "domestic partners" at city hall. This doesn't provide any substantial legal benefits, but it is a step forward in recognizing gay relationships.

Ironically, the argument generally used when people do not want to recognize a gay couple as having legal rights is that the couple is not legally married. Well, that's because it isn't legal for gay people to be married in this country. Without that certificate saying that a relationship is legal in the eyes of the courts, gay couples cannot successfully claim to be married.

However, there is increasing discussion about making gay marriages legal in the United States. Hawaii is the first state to consider legalizing gay unions, and the decision made there will have an enormous impact on gay rights. This would mean that gay couples can marry and have the same legal benefits and responsibilities as heterosexual couples. The courts then would have to recognize gay couples.

Anti-gay groups desperately do not want gay marriage to be legal. Why? Because it would mean admitting that gay relationships are as valid as are straight ones. It would mean acknowledging that gay women and men have equal rights and responsibilities. It would mean that gay couples could not be discriminated against in matters of housing, taxes, adoption, and many other things. Most importantly, it would mean admitting that there isn't just one way to be a family. That thought is very disturbing to many people, especially to members of the religious community. If gay marriages were legalized, churches will be forced to make serious decisions about whether or not those marriages will be seen as legal within the churches, and whether or not those marriages can be performed in the churches. That means rethinking thousands of years of teachings and going through endless arguments about the issue of homosexuality in general.

There are also people in the gay community who do not want to see gay marriages legalized. These people argue that making gay marriages legal would simply be imitating heterosexual life-styles, something gay people shouldn't do because it leads to all kinds of problems. They think it would be taking the worst traditions of straight life and forcing them on gay people, making the whole concept of having a life partner meaningless. They also point out that legalizing gay marriages might make it more difficult for unmarried gay couples to enjoy the same rights unless they too get married.

Other gay people are thrilled at the idea of legal gay marriages. They say that for the first time it makes our relationships equal with those of straight people in the eyes of the law. They argue that legalizing gay relationships might make gay people take their relationships more seriously, and that it makes issues like buying property and adopting children easier. They point out that seeing legalized gay relationships would make straight society have to rethink their ideas about gay people, and would also provide young people with positive role models.

While gay marriages are not currently legal under United States law, many churches do now perform marriage ceremonies for gay and lesbian couples. Many gay men and women hold wedding celebrations and exchange rings and vows in front of their friends and families. Many others hold private ceremonies for themselves to celebrate their relationships.

Regardless of whether or not gay marriage becomes legal, the point is that gay people have relationships just as straight people do, with most of the benefits and the drawbacks. We live together, buy homes together, break up, celebrate holidays, and go on vacations together as couples. We can spend years together as couples, and often do. Our families may or may not look like families in the traditional sense. They may be made up of many different kinds of friends with whom we celebrate holidays and special times. They may be made up of just ourselves and one other person. As gay people we learn to create many things for ourselves, even when we are told we can't have them.

We also have children. For years gay women and men who were married before they came out have raised their children from those marriages. Now more and more, gay people who were never married are choosing to raise children, either by having their own or through adoption. Both couples and single people are creating their own families by having kids.

Again, we do this in some nontraditional ways. Some lesbians ask a friend to father their children; others go to sperm banks and are fertilized there. Some gay men and lesbians have children together and share custody. Both gay men and lesbians adopt children, often from foreign countries. The definition of a family is a very broad one, and there is no one way or right way of creating a gay family.

How a gay person or couple chooses to start a family depends on many things. In some states it is very difficult for a gay person or a single person to adopt a child. Some people want to have their own biological children. It all depends on the person or couple choosing to have the child. What is important is that if we want children, we can have them. We don't have to give up the joys of having a family and children merely because we don't fit the standard definition of parents or a family.

The following books are about gay and lesbian parents and forming gay and lesbian families. Some are practical how-to guides that include information for people interested in starting a family, while others discuss some of the issues surrounding gay and lesbian parenting and adoption.

ARNUP, KATHERINE, ed., *Lesbian Parenting: Living with Pride & Prejudice* (Charlottetown, Canada: Gynergy, 1995).

BENKOV, LAURA, Ph.D., *The Lesbian and Gay Parents Handbook* (New York: HarperCollins, 1993).

BENKOV, LAURA, Ph.D., *Reinventing the Family* (New York: Crown, 1994).

CLUNIS, D. MERILEE AND G. DORSEY GREEN, *The Lesbian Parenting Book: A Guide to Creating Families and Raising Children* (Seattle, WA: Seal Press, 1995).

MANASSE, GEOFF AND JEAN SWALLOW, *Making Love Visible: In Celebration of Gay and Lesbian Families* (Freedom, CA: The Crossing Press, 1995).

MARTIN, APRIL, Ph.D., *The Lesbian and Gay Parenting Handbook: Creating and Raising Our Families* (New York: HarperCollins, 1993).

MORGAN, KENNETH B., *Getting Simon: Two Gay Doctors' Journey to Fatherhood* (New York: Bramble Books, 1995).

POLLACK, JILL S., *Lesbian and Gay Families: Redefining Parenting in America* (New York: Franklin Watts, 1995).

POLLACK, SANDRA AND JEANNE VAUGHAN, *Politics of the Heart: A Lesbian Parenting Anthology* (Ithaca, NY: Firebrand, 1987).

SEX: FOR WOMEN ONLY

What do I know about lesbian sex? Certainly not as much as I know about male gay sex. But I'm not here to give you a step-by-step guide to what women can do in bed. What I want to talk about is our ideas about sex, and maybe help you develop ideas of your own to think about.

For most people, sex conjures up heterosexual images of a man inserting his penis into a woman. Some people even think that's the *only* description of sex. Women in particular are conditioned to believe that without men they can't even have sex! It's as if without a penis in the room no one can do anything. Something a lot of people (especially men) ask about lesbians is, "But what can they do together?" Even some women wonder what two women could do together because, well, they think they just don't have all the parts.

Here's some good news. You don't need a penis to have sex. And you certainly don't need the man who's attached to the penis. There are a lot of things people can do to make love and feel good besides have heterosexual intercourse. All of these things are just as good as what most people think about when they think of sex. But people who want everyone to think that only sex involving a penis is real sex don't want you to know this. That's because it makes them afraid to think that two women could actually make love *without a man.*

The great thing about lesbian sex is that there is no right or wrong way to do it. There's no one thing that defines it, and there are no rules you have to follow when you do it. If you think about sex as being anything people can think of to do together, you can probably easily imagine what two women can do in bed. They can kiss, touch, lick, or rub each other. They can use their tongues, fingers, or sex toys to stimulate each other's bodies. They can do absolutely anything that feels good to them.

With no rules to follow, lesbians are free to explore many different kinds of sexual activity. What you should remember is that sex—any kind of sex—is about communication. When you have sex, it should be about exploring what feels good to you and what feels good to your partner. Sex isn't just bodies rubbing against each other; it's *minds* discovering what gets them excited. It's finding all of the wonderful ways in which you can make someone feel great about herself and how she can make you feel great about yourself. It's about learning what you like.

Women are often taught that taking pleasure from sex is shameful, or that enjoying sex makes them sluts or perverts. Nothing could be further from the truth. Your body is capable of experiencing great pleasure, and discovering that pleasure is perfectly healthy and natural. One of the many strange reasons homophobes give for "proving" that homosexuality is wrong is that gay people have sex because it feels good. Since people of the same sex can't make each other pregnant, then the reason we have sex is just because we enjoy it. People who are afraid of sex or afraid of gay people try to tell us that having fun and enjoying sex are bad things. Well, they're just plain wrong.

A big part of sex for many women is accepting how they look. We're all familiar with how women are taught from a very early age what women "should" look like to be sexually attractive to men, and we all know how these ridiculous images of women can make women feel bad about how they look. Well, lesbians are no exception.

Lesbians have issues about their body images just as straight women do. Women of all kinds worry about their weight and how they look. So do men. Lesbians, though, can sometimes have a rougher time of it because for years lesbians have been taught that they aren't "real" women and can't look the way real women look. You know the story: lesbians don't wear makeup or dresses and can't be pretty. They all have to have short hair and wear boring clothes and have short fingernails. Some of these thoughts even come from within the lesbian community itself. There are some lesbians who believe that wearing makeup and dresses is a sign of trying to fit in with straight society and that it's shameful to do so. They believe that lesbians should not wear those things, and they give other lesbians who do a hard time.

There are even words for how different lesbians like to look and act. Lesbians who look more masculine and don't wear typically feminine clothing are called "butches." Lesbians who wear makeup and dress in more feminine clothing are called "femmes." For many years, a lot of people assumed that butches were attracted sexually only to femmes, and that femmes were attracted only to butches. And often this was and still is true; but not always. Femme women can like other femme women, and butches can like other butches. Like the rest of lesbian sexuality, there are no rules about what you have to be or to whom you have to be attracted.

115

You can look and act any way you like. Not everyone has to look like k.d. lang, nor does everyone have to look like Melissa Etheridge. You can be heavy or thin, short or tall. You can have small breasts or large breasts, a shaved head or long hair. You can have a nose ring, tattoos, and a pierced lip, or you can wear dresses with combat boots. It doesn't matter. Women are attracted to lots of different types of women, and you don't have to make yourself look any special way for people to find you attractive.

A big part of lesbian sexuality is lesbian health. While AIDS has not had as big an impact on the lesbian community as it has on the gay male community, it is still something you should be aware of. We'll talk about AIDS in another chapter. Of more importance to lesbians are the issues of breast cancer and gynecological health. Every year many lesbians die from breast cancer and from cervical cancer because they have not educated themselves about women's health issues. Many lesbians also avoid going to doctors because they cannot afford to or because, like many women, they have been treated badly by doctors in the past. Because of this, cancers and other health problems that might be easily detected are not discovered until it is too late.

It probably seems strange to be talking about breast cancer and gynecological exams in a section about sex. But your physical health has a lot to do with your sexual health. It is important for you to understand how your body works and to have regular health exams. It's very easy to not go to the doctor or gynecologist for tests because it's unpleasant. But being in good physical health is crucial to your well-being, and you owe it to yourself to be healthy. Right now you may not be able to choose your own doctors, but someday you will be able to. When you do, there are many lesbian and non-lesbian doctors who are trained to treat the needs of lesbians.

When you become sexually active, don't expect to know everything all at once. Sex is something you work at learning about. While we all have some natural instincts for what makes us feel good, we also have to try different things and find out what we enjoy. Having sex is a learning process that goes on your whole life, so don't be in a hurry to know everything right away. As you start to discover what you like, you may find yourself wondering about other things or wanting to try things you might not have thought of before. That's great. It means your mind is opening up and that you're learning about who you are. Don't be afraid of this process or think that there's something wrong with you.

As you learn more about sex and what you like, you might find that there are things you enjoy doing or think about doing that other people tell you are strange. Even within the lesbian community there may be people who tell you that what you like isn't "right." There may be people who tell you that lesbians only have certain kinds of sex, and that anything else is wrong or abnormal.

For example, there are many lesbians who enjoy using dildos and other sex toys; there are also many who don't. There are many lesbians who enjoy sado-masochistic (S-M) sex, which might involve bondage, whipping, and other pleasure/pain activities. There are other women who feel S-M is degrading. Some lesbians enjoy role-playing sex games, and some like to use clothes in their sexual lives. There are many different ways of expressing yourself sexually.

The problem comes when anyone tries to say that a certain kind of sex is wrong. Lesbians do whatever they want to. No matter what anyone tells you, how you express yourself sexually is a good thing as long as it doesn't infringe on others. You might think no one else is interested in what you like. But the chances are that if you find something interesting and exciting, there are a lot of other women who do too.

When it comes to sex, the most important thing to remember is that you don't have to do it unless you want to. Your body is yours, and no one should be able to tell you what to do with it or when. If you don't want to have sex with someone, then don't do it. If you feel uncomfortable in a situation, get yourself out. Don't worry about what someone else might think about you if you say no. Your safety and well-being are more important than anyone's opinion of you.

If you have been sexually abused in any way, either physically or emotionally, you may find it very hard even to think about sex. Just the idea of someone else touching you might make you feel sick or terrified. If this is the case, then it's very important for you to find someone you can talk to about what has happened to you and how you feel about it. Sex is not a bad thing, and it's not wrong for you to enjoy. And if anyone has ever hurt you or forced you to have sex, it is in no way your fault, no matter what you may have been told. What's wrong is for someone to make you do something you don't want to.

Unfortunately, sexual abuse is very common, especially among young women. Many lesbians who were abused as young women spent years thinking that their lesbianism somehow caused the abuse. Besides being extremely emotionally damaging (and not at all true), this kind of pain can make just the idea of sex too much to handle. If you have experienced any form of abuse, you are not alone, and there are people who can be trusted to help you. If you are dealing with these kinds of issues, please tell someone who can help you, like a parent, a friend, a teacher, a coach, or anyone else you trust. If you don't know anyone, call your local lesbian and gay community center or one of the organizations listed at the back of the book. People who care are there to help you.

Sex should be something that you do because you want to, not because someone else tells you to do it or because you are doing it to try and make someone else love you. Enjoying sex does not make you a bad person, and loving yourself enough to find out what makes you happy is not being selfish. Exploring your sexuality, either by yourself or with other people, is something to enjoy and be proud of.

Having and enjoying sex is certainly not the only part of being a lesbian, but it can be a wonderful part. You deserve to know about sex and about what makes you happy sexually. Wanting to know about sex and wanting to have sex does not make you bad or strange or anything else. It means you're like most other people. If you are having sex already, you probably know how good it can be. If you haven't started yet, you have a lot of exciting experiences to look forward to.

THE BOSTON WOMEN'S HEALTH COLLECTIVE, *The New Our Bodies, Ourselves* (New York: Touchstone, 1992).

CASTER, WENDY, *The Lesbian Sex Book: A Guide for Women Who Love Women* (Boston: Alyson Publications, 1995).

MCCLURE, REGAN AND ANNE VESPRY, eds., *Lesbian Health Guide* (Toronto: Queer Press, 1994).

SCHRAMM-EVANS, ZOE, *Making Out: The Complete Book of Lesbian Sexuality* (San Francisco: HarperSanFrancisco, 1995).

TORONTO, ONTARIO — Michael Rowe

Toronto is the center of gay politics and culture in Canada with secondary centers in Montreal, Ottawa, and Vancouver. Gay and lesbian residents of other cities may take justifiable pride in their own hometowns and communities, but Torontonians are an especially proud breed. This is the city that people flock to from all over Canada to explore their gay sexuality in a sophisticated and tolerant environment. In terms of a wide and diverse community of gay men and lesbians, Toronto is without parallel anywhere else in Canada.

Situated on Lake Ontario, Toronto is a beautiful city, offering theater, restaurants, museums, shopping, music, and dance, along with a varied population. And Toronto is not plagued by a lot of the problems that can make cities unpleasant places to live. Violent crime is not a serious problem here, and the city is clean and well maintained. In fact, many people have described Toronto as a "clean" version of New York.

On the other hand, some people think that life in Toronto is a little too laid back. It's true that the atmosphere in the city is very relaxed, almost reserved, and people take things slowly. But for many men and women, including a large number of lesbian and gay people, Toronto is the best combination of big-city life and small neighborhood charm.

Toronto's "gay ghetto" or "gay village" is located minutes from the corner of Yonge and Bloor Streets, the center of downtown. The area, which is closed off for the annual June Pride Day to host the second largest Pride Day parade in North America (after San Francisco's), consists primarily of Church Street bordered by Wellesley Street and Carlton Street. This section of Church is peppered with bars and shops. It is not uncommon, of an evening, to see gay and lesbian couples of all ages strolling arm in arm along the street, greeting friends, or just having private moments together. Gawking straight passersby may make comments, but overt violence is rare in Toronto, and the strong gay presence in the neighborhood frequently acts as a deterrent. In the summer, drag shows can be enjoyed from the street, or through the open window of Bar 501 (at, 501 Church, naturally).

A first stop for a gay man or lesbian arriving in Toronto would probably be the Second Cup coffee shop at Church and Wellesley. The National Ballet School is one block over on Maitland, and many of the gay dance students stop into the coffee shop to meet friends for gossip and coffee. The primarily gay staff of the shop are friendly and knowledgeable about the area and its happenings and can offer some advice on what to do and where to go in the city. The smoking section in the back has lately become something of an unofficial gathering spot for gay teenagers in Toronto, many newly arrived in the city. The steps of the Second Cup were immortalized as "the steps" in several gay-oriented skits on the television comedy series *The Kids in the Hall.* They are a popular place for gays and lesbians to sit with a mug of coffee and watch the world go by.

As for meeting potential friends and lovers, Toronto is a city where it pays to go up and introduce yourself to someone you think you might like to meet. Torontonians aren't necessarily cold, but there is a sort of Canadian reserve in this city that can be a little intimidating to the uninitiated. Most people are eager to talk, however, and when the walls are broken down, people here are friendly. Once you start a conversation with someone, don't be surprised to have made a new friend.

Another excellent resource for people visiting the city or living here is the 519 Community Centre, the city's gay and lesbian community center. If Church Street is the crown of gay Toronto, this venerable institution is the jewel. It is a valuable source of practical information as well as a comfortable and accepting environment where there is usually someone to answer any questions you might have. It is a wonderful place to begin finding out about resources available to lesbian and gay people in the city.

The center also hosts the Lesbian, Gay, and Bisexual Youth of Toronto (LGBYT) support group. LGBYT provides peer support and a forum for people under twenty-six to discuss a wide range of issues in a safe and confidential environment. LGBYT meets every Tuesday evening at 8:30 P.M. in the auditorium for topic discussion, and every Saturday at 1:00 P.M. in the Cawthra Cafe (located at the center) for an informal drop-in called "Alternatives." LGBYT has two branch groups: a women's group that meets on Tuesday evenings at 7:30, and a Newcomer's group that meets at 8:00 P.M. for people who have been with LGBYT for three weeks or less. This group is also recommended for those young people who are "freshly out" and who are seeking less politically charged information.

For gay young people the city also recently launched the pilot program for a gay, lesbian, and bisexual high school called the Triangle Program in the basement of the Metropolitan Community Church on Simpson Avenue, one block east of Broadview and Gerrard.

Toronto's three major universities (University of Toronto, Ryerson Polytechnical University, and York University) and many community colleges each have gay student organizations, many of which sponsor dances and meetings, and support gay-oriented cultural and social subgroups.

To find out about the goings-on in gay Toronto, pick up copies of the city's two major gay magazines: *Xtra!*, a tabloid-size newsmagazine featuring excellent reviews and articles, and *Fab!*, a small, elegant, glossy magazine specializing in fashion, humor, and club news. Toronto's gay-centered bars, clubs, restaurants, and support groups are all listed in the magazines, both of which are free and are found in most stores, bars, and clubs.

Xtra!'s Xtension page lists all of Toronto's gay groups and provides a convenient touch-tone method for reaching them. *Xtra!*'s listings also cover numerous religious (MCC, Congregation Keshet Shalom, Dignity), ethnic (Two-Spirited People of the First Nations, South Asian

Gay Men of Toronto, T.O.R.A. Greek Gays and Lesbians, Arabic Women's Solidarity Associations), hobby (Classical Music Club, Singing Out! The Lesbian and Gay Chorus of Toronto, Triangle Squares Square Dancing, Star Trek Fan Club-USS *Endeavour*), and athletic (Downtown Swim Club, Frontrunners, Gay and Lesbian Rowing Club) groups.

Another excellent source of information about meeting groups, film festivals, poetry readings, and the cultural arena is the bulletin board outside the Glad Day bookstore on Yonge Steet. The bookstore also stocks the best and widest selection of gay and lesbian books and periodicals anywhere in Canada.

Toronto tends to respect diversity within its gay community, and mutual regard is a byword here. Once you meet a few people, they can introduce you to more of their friends, and before you know it, the city feels more like a small town where it's not only OK but actually *advantageous* to be exactly who and what you are.

MICHAEL ROWE is an award-winning freelance journalist. He writes frequently for a variety of magazines, and his work has appeared in the anthologies Sister and Brother: Lesbians and Gay Men Write about Their Lives Together, Friends and Lovers: Gay Men Write about the Families They Create, *and others. The editor of* Writing Below the Belt: Conversations with Erotic Authors, *he lives with his life partner in Toronto.*

SEX: FOR MEN ONLY

A lot of people believe that all gay men think only about having sex. They believe that being gay means having a perfect body and having sex with as many men as possible (and for some men, that is what it means). But for most of us, sex is just another part of our lives. It doesn't define us, and we don't make it the most important thing in the world. But whatever sex means to us, gay guys have some issues about sex that are different from the issues lesbians have. Some of these are the same issues straight guys have, but some of them are ours alone.

A major issue for gay men is body image. What does this mean? It means we're hung up about how we look. We might think we don't have enough muscles, that our hair or eyes are the "wrong" color, or that we're too heavy. A lot of guys also worry about how big their penises are. All of these things are part of our body image, and all of them can contribute to how we see ourselves sexually.

As gay men, a lot of the images we see of other gay men come from magazines or from advertising aimed at gay men. If you've ever seen a gay magazine, you've probably noticed that the people depicted are almost always young, muscular guys who have perfect bodies and beautiful faces. They look as if they spend seven hours a day at the gym.

A lot of gay men are very concerned with trying to achieve the "perfect look." They believe that the only way they will be popular, have friends, find lovers, and be accepted as gay men is if they look like the guys in the pictures they see. This kind of thinking is very dangerous. It makes us worry more about how we look on the outside than about who we are on the inside. It's fine to want to have a muscular body and to look good, but it's not fine if you want it only because you think it's how you get guys to notice you.

Part of enjoying sex is learning to be happy with how you look. This doesn't mean it's bad to want to try different things with your hair or lose some weight or build up your muscles. It means understanding that you don't have to have the perfect build to be an attractive person other guys will want to be with. It means trying not to worry so much about what clothes you wear or what other people think of how you look. It means not basing your self-worth, or the worth of others, on whether or not you or they look like the guys you might see in magazines or in movies.

When it comes to having sex, gay men have a couple of things to think about. Foremost is AIDS (which we'll talk about later in another chapter). It's easy to be scared of AIDS, and you should be concerned about it, but there are ways to protect yourself. Understanding what AIDS is and how it is and is not spread is a big part of educating yourself about sex.

Another thing guys worry about is exactly what two guys do during sex. The good news is that they do anything they want to. Sex doesn't have to be doing things from a list. It's anything you want it to be. Sex between men can involve touching each other, masturbating yourselves or each other, kissing, licking or sucking each other's penises, and anything else you can think of.

For many guys, the biggest concern about sex is often anal intercourse. Yet this is just one part of what making love can be. It's certainly not the only or even the most important part. But it's what a lot of people think about when they think of two men having sex. Many gay men worry about this issue. We worry about if we'll know how to do it, about whether it will hurt if someone does it to us, and whether we'll like it.

But anal sex can be a very enjoyable part of sex. Most people worry about it for nothing. If you take your time to learn how to do it, it can make the whole thing less frightening. How do you learn? You start by learning about your anus. Most of us only think about our anuses (the opening to the rectum) in terms of getting rid of waste. But the anus can also be a sensual orifice. There are many nerves in this part of your body, and rubbing it with your fingers can be very exciting.

If you try rubbing your anus with your fingers and try to relax your body, you will find that you can probably insert your finger fairly easily. The anus is actually the opening of a ring of muscle called the sphincter, and this is what you feel tighten around your finger if you try to insert your finger. When people have pain during anal sex, it's usually because the sphincter muscle is not relaxed. If you learn to relax this muscle, you can learn to enjoy anal sex. You can easily practice putting your finger or fingers inside your anus and learning how to relax your sphincter muscle. If it's too tight and hurts, you can try using a lubricant such as K-Y Jelly on your fingers to make them slippery. Do not try to insert anything sharp or pointed into your rectum or you might cause bleeding.

A lot of guys worry needlessly about anal sex. Apart from worrying that having someone's penis inside our bodies will hurt, we worry that we will have to have a bowel movement during sex. We worry that putting our penises in someone else's body will be dirty. The fact is, if you learn how your body works and practice understanding your body, anal sex can be very pleasurable.

With any sex act, don't worry about whether or not you "should" like it. Some guys like giving anal sex; some guys like getting anal sex; most like both. Some guys like to lick and suck someone's penis; other guys like to have their penises licked and sucked; most like both. If you find you don't like something, don't worry about it. You don't have to like everything.

On the other hand, don't think that because you do or do not like something that it makes you any better than someone else. For example, many gay men worry that if they like getting anal sex that it means that they are less masculine. Or they think that men who give anal sex are somehow more masculine than men who don't. We even have words for this. We say that men who give anal sex are "tops" and that men who like to get anal sex are "bottoms."

The first time I heard someone mention tops and bottoms, I was really confused. I thought they were talking about clothes. I had no idea it meant what kind of sex someone liked to have. The whole notion of tops and bottoms can be upsetting to men, especially young men, because basically it can make guys who like getting anal sex feel they are playing the role women usually play in heterosexual sex. Guys worry that if they like getting anal sex that it somehow makes them the "woman" in sex.

This is a ridiculous idea, and insults everyone, especially women! You really shouldn't worry about it. Someone who likes to give anal sex is no more masculine than someone who likes to get anal sex. Most guys like both parts. But people who are insecure about who they are may say, "I'm only a top" because they think it makes them more powerful or controlling. Similarly, a guy may let other guys suck his penis but he won't suck theirs. He thinks he's still being a "real man" because he isn't really doing anything gay.

Don't let attitudes like this determine what you do sexually. If you like how something feels, then do it. Don't worry about whether it makes you more or less of a man. What really makes you less of a man is thinking that you are any better than someone else because of what you do or how you do it. Once you realize that all forms of sex are good, then you free yourself up to enjoy all kinds of things.

Gay men have a wide range of sexualities. Some men like to use sex toys. Some enjoy watching pornographic movies. Others are partial to leather, uniforms, and other fetishes. A number of gay men are involved in pleasure/pain activities. All of these are ways of expressing ourselves sexually, and all of them are valid. Just as there is no one way to be as a person, there is no one way to have sex.

Similarly, there is no one way to be a gay man when it comes to sex. Some gay men have lots of sex with lots of different partners; others stay with one person for their whole lives. Most of us fall somewhere in the middle. Unfortunately, as gay men, we are not taught to form relationships with other men, and because of this a lot of us spend our lives moving from person to person, looking for sex partners to fill an emotional need. For some people this works just fine, but for others it results in feelings of loneliness and depression. Sometimes as gay men it's easy to feel as if having sex with as many people as possible is a requirement of being gay. It's important to know that there are other options available as well.

Having to deal with things like AIDS and with all of our different feelings about sex can make it seem like it's not worth the effort. But it is. The important thing is to just take your time and not get too stressed out about when you have sex or what you do. You'll find out soon enough what you like, what you don't like, and what you might want to try. Don't do anything you don't want to, and don't let people pressure you into doing things you're not ready for.

HART, JACK, *My First Time: Gay Men Describe Their First Same-Sex Experiences* (Boston: Alyson Publications, 1995).

TATCHELL, PETER, *Safer Sexy: The Guide to Gay Sex Safely* (London: Freedom Editions, 1994).

WALKER, MITCH, *Men Loving Men: A Gay Guide & Consciousness Book* (San Francisco, CA: Gay Sunshine Press, 1994).

SILVERSTEIN, DR. CHARLES AND FELICE PICANO, *The New Joy of Gay Sex* (New York: HarperCollins, 1992).

SARA MOON: MOTHER AND GARDENER

"When I came out, it was very tough," recalls Sara Moon, a gardener. "I came out at fourteen, and my family didn't handle it at all well. They told me to leave the house and never come back." Devastated by this reaction, Sara went to live with her maternal grandmother, who supported Sara and tried to make peace in the family. "She tried very hard to help me," says Sara, "but my parents, my father especially, couldn't understand what my being a lesbian meant. He kept asking me why I couldn't just be 'normal.'"

Of Sioux Indian and African-American descent, Sara faced disapproval from both sides of her family. Not welcome at family gatherings, for the next seven years she had contact with only a handful of relatives. Despite repeated attempts to reconcile with her parents, every discussion ended in an argument. Finally, she decided to move away from her family entirely. "Sometimes the best thing to do is to just go," she says. "It's extremely hard to do, but saving your sanity is more important than trying to make other people happy. I was going crazy wondering what *I* had done wrong, rather than just accepting that *they* were wrong."

Relocating to the East Coast, Sara found a welcoming lesbian community in western Massachusetts, where she continues to live. "It really felt like coming home," she said. "For the first time in years I felt as if I had a real family of people who understood what I was feeling, what I was going through. All of that time growing up I felt that there must be something about me that just wasn't right, that I just didn't belong anywhere. Now I had a whole group of people who had all been through similar experiences."

Sara also met Elizabeth, her partner of the last twelve years. Elizabeth, a high school English teacher, and Sara are the mothers of a little girl, now seven. Alice's father is a gay man with whom Sara and Elizabeth remain close friends, but who is not involved in raising Alice. "I always wanted a child," Sara says. "Because I'm a lesbian, I assumed that I

couldn't have one. You know, that's one of the worst things we're taught to believe about ourselves as gay people. As a woman I think I especially felt bad because I felt like I was being told that because of my sexuality I wasn't a real woman. The implication was that I wasn't able to give birth simply because I love other women instead of men."

Having a child has helped Sara heal some of the pain caused by the separation from her parents. While her father died several years ago, she now has some contact with her mother. "I think becoming a grandmother softened her somewhat," Sara says. "We will never have what I consider a mother/daughter relationship, and there is a lot of pain I still deal with, but at least we can have conversations now, as long as the 'L' word never comes up. We stick to talking about Alice, which is a fairly safe topic as long as I agree with everything she says. I think she feels awful about what happened, but she doesn't know how to make up for it or even discuss it. So in many ways we both just pretend it never happened. I suppose a therapist would have a field day with that, but that's the way it is."

Raising Alice has also taught Sara a great deal about how people perceive gays and lesbians. "When Alice was two, Elizabeth and I moved for two years to another town while Elizabeth was getting her master's degree," she recalls. "The people there had just never seen anything like this, two women raising a child. Especially two women of different colors with a child that didn't really look like either of them. We got a lot of funny stares and even funnier questions. There were some mean things said too, about how queers shouldn't have kids and whatnot. But what we generally found was that if we just acted ourselves, the people who didn't like us went away when they saw that we weren't afraid of them."

This practical approach is something Sara thinks more lesbian and gay people need to take. "You know, life is always going to be challenging. There are always going to be people who give you a hard

time about something, whether it's how you look, what you do, or if you're two women raising a child. You can't not do things because you're afraid of how people will react. One of the big problems we have in the gay community is people worrying about how other people—straight people—will react to certain things. Yes, homophobia exists. Yes, people still hate gay people. But you know what, there will always be people like that. There will always be homophobes and bigots. And the way to fight those people is to just live our lives. Marching and shaking our fists has its place, but the strongest statement we can make is to just be who we are."

A gardener by profession, Sara started her own business after tiring of a job in the professional world. "I worked as a copywriter at an ad agency in Boston for a few years," she says. "It was OK, but I really wanted to do something that I felt was more useful, more part of who I am as a person. After one too many days of extolling the virtues of feminine hygiene products and diet soft drinks, I decided to do something I loved." Today she designs and plants gardens for a number of clients, which include individuals as well as local restaurants. "This business is great," she says. "I work with straight people, but a lot of my clients are also gay, and it makes me feel as if I'm giving something to the community, keeping it in the family, as it were."

Community is important to Sara, who spends much of her free time volunteering for a number of organizations, including a women's health center and a program for lesbian and gay teens. "What I went through as a teenager had an impact on me," she says sadly. "I remember all too well feeling worthless and ashamed. Unfortunately, there are still a lot of young people who go through that. There are still a lot of young gay people whose parents throw them out of the house, or who feel suicidal. The suicide rate for lesbian and gay teens is three times what it is for straight teens. Someone has to start reaching these kids. Having been through all of those things, I can tell the kids I work with that I know what it's like. I can also show them, just by being there, that life changes, that things do get better with time."

Asked about what she thinks the gay community needs to do for itself, Sara says, "I think one major thing we need to do is start working together more. There are so many divisions right now. Women and men don't work together. People of color often feel left out. People grumble about bisexuals. People without kids don't relate to those who have kids. There are all of these different groups within the community, which is good, but we have to learn how to find common ground if we want to really accomplish anything. My advice to people becoming involved in their local communities is to learn about other people's issues. See what other people are concerned about, even if it doesn't seem to affect you. Because once we start treating each other like a family should, which means supporting one another, then we'll create a place where we can all feel at home."

AIDS

Perhaps nothing else in history has changed life for gay people the way the AIDS crisis has. Since its initial appearance in the early 1980s, AIDS has swept through the gay community, taking millions of lives and leaving people frightened and afraid. Just the thought of AIDS terrifies people, and for young gay people facing a future in which AIDS is an inevitable fact of life, it seems like the most awful thing that has ever happened.

You do not have to be afraid of AIDS. You have to know how to avoid it, and you have to know the facts about it, but you do not have to be afraid of it. Why? Because it is completely within your power to remain free from AIDS. And the way you do that is by educating yourself about what AIDS is, how you get it, and how you don't get it.

Here's what AIDS isn't: It is not a "gay disease," and it is not a punishment for being gay. Because gay men were the first visible examples of people with AIDS in the United States, many people believed that only gay men got it. Some people said this was God's wrath against homosexuals and that gay men deserved to get AIDS because they had "abnormal" sex. But AIDS affects both straight and gay people. It affects women and men, white and black, rich and poor people. It is an equal opportunity disease. No one group "started" AIDS, and no one group is solely responsible for its spread. Men can spread it to women. Women can spread it to men. And both women and men can spread it to people of the same sex.

AIDS is a disease that causes your immune system, which helps to fight off diseases, not to work properly; your body cannot fight off viruses and infections, and you become sick. AIDS is caused by a virus called the human immunodeficiency virus (HIV). People don't just get AIDS: people become infected with HIV, which over a period of time leads to AIDS by destroying the cells in the body that fight off infections. What we are really saying when we talk about preventing AIDS is preventing ourselves from being infected by HIV. If you aren't infected with HIV, you can't get AIDS.

HIV works by getting into your bloodstream. That is the only way it works. Unlike other viruses, such as the cold and flu viruses, HIV cannot infect you just because someone sneezes on you, coughs on you, or kisses you. You cannot become infected with HIV by sharing glasses or dishes with someone who has it. HIV has to enter your blood directly in order to affect you. This can happen in several ways, and all of them involve your blood coming into contact with someone else's body fluids.

HIV is always found in the body fluids of an infected person. These fluids are semen, vaginal secretions, breast milk, and blood. Yes, HIV is found in saliva, but most scientists believe that it is not present in significant enough amounts for you to worry about. You really only have to worry about the four main fluids listed above. And you only have to worry about their getting into your blood. HIV infection occurs *only* when infected blood, semen, vaginal fluids, and breast milk enter your body and come into contact with your bloodstream. The virus then passes from the infected body fluid into your blood.

The easiest way to become infected with HIV is to use tainted needles to inject drugs, steroids, or any other substances. When a needle that may have come into contact with someone else's blood is pushed into your body, HIV can get right into your bloodstream because it can remain on the needle after being removed from someone else. It's just like injecting yourself with HIV. Related ways of becoming infected are to get tattooed or pierced with dirty needles or to rub open cuts on your body together with open cuts on someone else's body, as some people do in blood oaths when joining gangs or symbolizing friendships.

All donated blood and organs today in the United States are tested for HIV, so there is little chance of being infected through blood transfusions or organ transplants. And almost all instances of infection through breast milk are from infected mothers to their newborn babies, not from adults to adults (although I suppose it's possible to become infected if you drink infected breast milk).

For gay people, the main means of transmission is sex, and this is the most important area to be educated about when it comes to AIDS. While instances of new cases of HIV infection have dropped in gay men over the age of twenty-five, one of the groups in which new cases are increasing is gay men under twenty-five. So for young gay men, this is a crucial issue. Another group that is seeing an increase in new cases of HIV infection is women under twenty-five. While almost all sexually related cases of infection in women are from heterosexual sex, women can pass the virus to other women, so it is important for lesbians to know about AIDS.

HIV is *always* found in semen and vaginal fluids if someone is infected. This means that if you come into contact with these fluids, you are exposing yourself to HIV. Remember, though, that the infected fluid has got to come into direct contact with your bloodstream. This happens in several ways.

In anal sex between men, one partner puts his penis into the rectum of the other. This means that his penis and any fluids that come out of it are coming into contact with the walls of the other partner's rectum. These fluids can be semen or "precome," the clear sticky fluid produced by a man's penis before ejaculation. The walls of the rectum are very thin, and it is easy to scrape or tear them. While this doesn't normally cause problems (unless the tear is severe), it does mean that any HIV in an infected partner's semen or precome has a direct door into the other partner's bloodstream.

Some men believe that it's OK to have unprotected anal sex as long as the partner pulls out before he comes. This isn't really true, because HIV is also found in precome, which can leak from the penis without anyone even knowing it. Beyond that, trusting someone to pull out before he comes is a risky thing to do. It's very easy for someone to get carried away by sex and to forget to pull out or just not be able to control himself.

The most controversial issue for most gay men when talking about AIDS is oral sex. What is the likelihood of AIDS transmission during oral sex? If the person doing the sucking has any cuts or scrapes on his tongue or gums, it may be possible for HIV contained in the semen and precome to enter his bloodstream through these cuts. It may also be possible for HIV to pass from any blood in an infected person's mouth through scrapes or cuts on the penis of the man whose penis is being sucked. So in oral sex, both partners are potentially at risk.

Again, many men believe that as long as you stop sucking someone's penis before he comes in your mouth that it's safe. Others say that getting even tiny amounts of precome or semen in your mouth is dangerous. There is really no agreement. The fact is, HIV can enter your bloodstream through cuts or scrapes in your mouth; and semen and precome contain HIV. So if infected semen or precome is in your mouth, and you have cuts, then you could possibly be infected. No one knows how big the cuts have to be, how much semen you have to come into contact with, or what the real danger is of being infected with HIV through oral sex. But the fact is that, at least theoretically, it could happen.

Often when we talk about AIDS we don't talk about issues for lesbians because lesbians with AIDS are not a visible group the way men with AIDS are. But it is possible for women to transmit HIV to one another. The most likely way for this to happen is during oral sex. If the woman who is receiving the oral sex is infected with HIV, it is possible for the virus to enter small cuts in or on her partner's mouth and tongue if they come into contact with her infected vaginal fluids. It may also be possible for the woman receiving oral sex to become infected if her partner has open cuts on her tongue or gums and infected blood passes from her mouth into her partner's vagina. This blood can enter the bloodstream through any cuts or scrapes in the thin vaginal walls.

Some lesbians are also concerned that HIV could be passed from one person to another through cuts on the fingers or cuticles of the fingernails during sexual activity where one woman's fingers are inside another woman's vagina. And there is also the possibility of transmitting HIV when vibrators or other things that are inserted into the vagina during sex are used by one person and then shared with another. This is because vaginal fluids will stick to the object and then come into direct contact with the other partner's vaginal walls.

So now that you know how HIV can be spread, what do you need to know to prevent being infected? Luckily, that's really easy. The way to prevent being infected with HIV is to prevent coming into contact with it. For men that means using condoms during sex. For women it means using pieces of latex rubber called dental dams.

Latex condoms are at present the best protection against HIV. The virus cannot pass through the latex, so it cannot reach any cuts that might be on your body. This is not true of condoms made of animal products like lambskin, so make sure the rubbers you use are only latex rubber. You should use a rubber any time you have anal sex, and it's recommended for oral sex too. This way, if someone comes while his penis is in your mouth or in your rectum, the semen will be trapped inside the rubber and can't reach you to infect you. If you are the person who is getting his penis sucked or putting his penis into someone else's rectum, a rubber will also prevent you from coming into contact with any infected body fluids the other person might have.

Condoms are not hard to use. All you have to do is roll one onto your penis and run your fingers down the sides to push out any air that is trapped inside. If the condom doesn't have a special tip for semen to collect in, you should also leave a little room at the end. This way, when you come, you won't break the condom. If you are using any kind of lubricant with your condom (and you should for anal sex), make sure it is a water-based lubricant like K-Y Jelly. Do not use lubricants that are oil-based, like Crisco or vegetable oil. They can cause latex to break. With a little practice, using condoms during sex can be very easy.

As usual, women don't have it so easy. It is suggested that women use dental dams during oral sex. Dental dams are small squares of rubber (usually sold at drugstores near the dental floss and toothbrushes) that are used when dentists need to protect part of the mouth during dental procedures. The way you use dental dams for oral sex is by spreading them over your partner's vagina and holding them in place while you run your tongue over the area.

However, dental dams are hard to find, and most women find dental dams to be almost impossible to use because they aren't very big and it's tricky to hold them in place. A much easier method is to use a big piece of plastic wrap to make a barrier between your mouth and your partner's vagina. Just don't use the kind with air holes in it. You can also make a dental dam by taking a condom, cutting it down one side with scissors, and opening it to make a larger square of latex.

For protecting yourself during sex where your fingers are inside your partner's vagina, you can wear latex gloves. These you can usually find in a drugstore. Believe it or not, using gloves can actually be a lot of fun. Even people who don't need to practice safer sex find using them can be a real turn-on. If you are having sex that involves using things that are inserted into the vagina or rectum, you can play safely by covering the object with a condom. That way, if you are sharing it with someone, you can change the condom before moving from one person to another.

AIDS, unless someone is very sick with it, is an invisible disease. You can't tell someone has it just by looking at him or her. Don't assume someone is not infected just because he says so, because she seems so pretty, or because you're horny and want to have sex. You can't tell by looking at someone how many people he's slept with and whether any one of them was infected with HIV. It only takes one exposure to HIV to become infected, and once you are you can't get rid of it. As a gay young person, you are accountable for yourself. You will probably be exploring a lot of different things sexually, and it is your responsibility to know what risks are involved when you go to bed with someone.

More than anything, having responsible sex means caring about yourself enough to know what you will do and what you won't do. Most young gay men who become infected with HIV say that they knew the facts about HIV. They knew that if they had unprotected sex, they could be infected. But they chose to do it anyway. Why? Many say it's because they have heard so many stories about how easy and free sex used to be for gay men and they wanted to see what it was like. Many say they wanted someone to like them, so they let him have unprotected sex with them. And others say they did it because they just didn't care.

Sex is great—but it isn't worth dying for. Yes, sex for gay men used to be a lot easier. But it was no better. It was just different. We still have sex, but now we have to stop and put a condom on first, or we

10 THINGS YOU CAN DO TO FIGHT AIDS

1. **FIND OUT** what AIDS is

2. **VOLUNTEER** at an AIDS organization

3. **ASK** someone to speak to your local school about AIDS

4. **PARTICIPATE** in an AIDS walk-a-thon or other fund-raising event

5. **EDUCATE** your friends about AIDS

6. **BECOME** a buddy to someone living with AIDS

7. **DONATE** money to AIDS organizations

8. **PRACTICE** safer sex

9. **FIND OUT** if your local school has an AIDS education program or condom distribution program

10. **INFORM** yourself about AIDS issues and stay informed

have to think before we go home with someone. But after that the sex is just as good. And letting someone have unprotected sex with you isn't making that person like you. It's telling that person that you don't respect yourself enough to make him respect you by wearing a condom. Real respect is knowing that your life is worth a lot more than a few minutes of pleasure.

Strange as it may sound, there are some gay men who believe that becoming infected with HIV will make them part of the gay world, or others who believe that they'll get it anyway so they might as well not worry about safe sex. This is just about the stupidest thing anyone could ever think. The only thing becoming HIV-positive will make you is sick. It won't make you part of a special group. AIDS does not have to be inevitable. It is totally up to you whether or not you become infected, so pretending that it's fate is really dumb. No one has to get AIDS. People choose to get AIDS when they don't use condoms or when they say yes to risky activities. We know enough about AIDS now that there is no reason for anyone else to become infected with HIV.

Many of us have grown up with AIDS as part of our world. Unless a miracle happens, it will probably be around our entire lives. This doesn't mean it has to rule your life. It just means that some parts of your life may have to adapt to accommodate AIDS. You may have to be more careful about what you do and who you do it with. You may have to make some hard choices that gay people before you didn't have to make. But AIDS isn't only a gay issue. People of all kinds will be making these same choices. So don't think that you're being punished for being gay or that AIDS is something that makes being gay harder. We all have to live with it in our lives.

Reading all of this, you may feel as though everyone out there has AIDS and that you can never have sex without putting on seventeen layers of protection. It's not that bad. The reality is that we all now live in a time when AIDS is a big concern, and one that we can't afford to ignore. It's true that the times when people had sex without worrying about anything deadly are over.

But sex isn't dead. You can still have exciting sex and be safe. It just takes a little more planning than it used to. Carry condoms with you. Know how to use them properly. Know what the risks are for different kinds of sexual activity and make smart choices based on what you know.

Find out about AIDS. Know what it is and what it isn't. Don't let yourself think you're too young, too smart, too good, or that it doesn't matter. Educate yourself about safer sex and about health issues. Your greatest protection against AIDS, or any disease, is knowing the facts.

A simple, handy book that answers many common questions about HIV/AIDS is my book *100 Questions and Answers about AIDS: What You Need to Know Now* (New York: Beech Tree Books, 1994).

ST. LOUIS, MISSOURI — Jim Thomas

As the mood of a city goes, so goes the lesbian and gay community. The democracy of any gay and lesbian community is perhaps its most apparent feature; we are everywhere and come from every portion of our larger communities. And so, looking at a city's larger community, it is generally a safe bet that the lesbian and gay community within is pretty similar.

This is as true in St. Louis as it is anywhere else. A large industrial city beset by its share of urban troubles, struggling sometimes to hold together, there are still quiet victories and surprising pleasures to be found in St. Louis. Named after a king known for religious tolerance, and dominated in its religious culture by the Catholic Church, there is almost no radical right activism in St. Louis, its conservatism grounded in orthodoxy rather than radicalism. The image of the fist-shaking conservative Midwest is misleading: Most Midwesterners are solidly live and let live.

The result can be an atmosphere of frustrating complacency for those of the activist bent, but one of comforting safety for those looking for ease of everyday living without a lot of fuss and bother. What one perhaps loses in the lack of the gay trendsetting culture seen in some other cities, one gains in life's more daily concerns. In many ways that are important, St. Louis is a very easy city in which to live, with accessible institutions and an inexpensive cost of living. The gay and lesbian community here goes about its business quietly, blending into the rest of the city and living quietly and happily alongside its straight neighbors.

The gay and lesbian community is largely concentrated in the central corridor, a set of neighborhoods beginning at the Gateway Arch on the river downtown and heading more or less west through the city and county: Soulard, the oldest extant neighborhood in the city, with strong French architectural gestures and a wonderful farmer's market; Lafayette Square, the city's first fashionable rich neighborhood, with grand homes lovingly restored and some of the best new fill-in construction to be found anywhere; the Shaw neighborhood, next to the wonderful Missouri Botanical Gardens and Tower Grove Park, with its bustling business district on South Grand; the Central West End, filled with private streets and sidewalk cafés; and the Delmar Loop, the most bohemian of the neighborhoods because of its proximity to Washington University. None of these neighborhoods are "gay" in the classic sense, for example, of a Castro (in San Francisco) or a Greenwich Village, but they are comfortable enclaves stretched like a necklace across the city.

Of the surrounding communities, Alton to the north at the conjunction of three great rivers—Illinois, Missouri, and Mississippi—has perhaps the most visible gay and lesbian community. Known lately as the hub of great floods, the bluff city has old charming neighborhoods on hills above the river. Other cities in nearby Illinois with bars and some semblance of community are Granite City and Belleville. There are bars in East St. Louis, but though improving, it is still perhaps the most dangerous city in the entire metropolitan area. Don't go unless you are with someone who already knows the way.

There are two publications serving the gay community in St. Louis. The *News-Telegraph* is a traditional tabloid newspaper, publishing semimonthly (but soon to go weekly). It is the best place to turn for news, analysis, features, and a community calendar. *TWISL*, also publishing semimonthly in a magazine format, is the social paper and the better source for information on what is happening in the gay community. Because of the casual nature of the St. Louis gay community, many social events involve friends getting together, rather than large, organized activities.

There is no gay community center in St. Louis, although at this writing there is talk of forming one. The organizing group does run a voice message system for local organizations, which can be reached at (314) 997-9897. While far from ideal, this can be a good way to contact many of the groups in town.

There are two bookstores in St. Louis that provide some of the functions usually associated with a community center. Our World Too at 11 S. Vandeventer (314-533-5322) is the city's true gay and lesbian bookstore, catering exclusively to the community. It has a meeting room used by various support groups, and its bulletin board is one of the best places to get basic information on organizations and upcoming events. The store carries everything from magazines to classic English poetry, and features the latest in gay and lesbian reading material.

Growing American Youth (GAY), which holds special meetings for young people, meets at Our World Too. GAY is one of the oldest youth support groups around, and has a strong supporter in the owner of the store. The group can be contacted by calling the store, and it is also a very good and safe place for anyone under the age of eighteen looking for a starting place in the community.

Left Bank Books at 399 N. Euclid (314-367-6731) is a general bookstore, but is jointly owned by a gay man and a lesbian and features books of interest to gay readers. It may well be the best bookstore in town, and is very gay- and lesbian-friendly. It also runs a great coffeehouse next door.

A variety of denominational groups in St. Louis, including the gay Catholic group Dignity, help in meeting some of the social as well as the religious needs of the city's gay and lesbian community.

As befits the neighborhood patterns, the gay bars in St. Louis are not located in any one area, but are scattered, with one or two exceptions, throughout the central corridor. While there are not the numbers of bars found in larger cities, there is a diversity of settings and places where anyone may feel comfortable, from women to leathermen to disco dancers. The bars have tended to remain stable over the last several years, and any of the guidebooks to gay places in St. Louis can point you to the atmosphere of your choice.

There is a thriving athletic community in St. Louis, and joining sports teams is a good way to become involved in gay social life here. There is, among others, a women's and a coed softball league, a volleyball organization, a bowling league, and a chapter of Frontrunners for joggers. Team St. Louis does an excellent job of organizing the state team for the Gay Games and has regularly brought home medals from this international event.

Politically, the lead organization in town is the Privacy Rights Education Project, which, as its name implies, works to educate people about privacy issues. The Missouri Task Force for Lesbian and Gay Concerns, also situated here, is the state organization. The gay organizations in nearby Illinois are all organized in Chicago, and except for the Illinois Federation for Human Rights, they have no presence at all in the Illinois part of the St. Louis area. Both of the St. Louis groups are mostly focused on community building, as there is little gay-related activity coming from the state legislature to address, and the city already has passed a civil rights law that includes sexual orientation.

In fact, that antidiscrimination law is perhaps representative of the paradoxes in St. Louis life. The law was passed quietly and unanimously during an otherwise routine revision of city nondiscrimination laws. Most of the gay community were not even aware of it! The passage was realized when an activist went to City Hall to get a copy of the law to study up on how to amend it. When the clerk discovered why he was there, she informed him he was too late: gays and lesbians were already protected (and we didn't even know it). (A mild controversy ensued in which it became clear that out of twenty-eight members of the board of aldermen, only one changed his position to oppose the measure.)

So it goes in this conservative city, that we got our nondiscrimination ordinance without lifting a finger, in perhaps the easiest political non-effort for such a law ever seen in the nation.

It's a quiet city in style and tone, but it does have its moments.

✪

JIM THOMAS, cofounder and managing editor of the News-Telegraph, *has been involved in the lesbian and gay community for many years at both the national and local levels. In 1979 he was on the national steering committee of the National March on Washington for Lesbian and Gay Rights. He was founding chair in 1980 of the St. Louis Lesbian and Gay Pride Celebration, and has served on the boards of the ACLU (Eastern Missouri) and the National Gay and Lesbian Task Force. He began the process that eventually led to the founding of the Missouri Task Force for Lesbian and Gay Concerns. He is also a member of the Political Action Committee of the National Abortion and Reproductive Rights Action League/Missouri and is chair of the National Community Advisory Board of the AIDS Vaccine Evaluation Group. He also plays viola in the St. Louis Philharmonic Orchestra.*

BISEXUALITY

Most of us understand what it means to be gay or to be lesbian. We know that gay men are attracted emotionally, physically, and mentally to men, and that lesbians are women who are attracted in the same way to other women. But sometimes things aren't always that clear. Some people find that sometimes they are attracted to men and other times they are attracted to women. This can be really confusing, because we are conditioned to think that people are either gay or they are straight. We don't usually talk about other possibilities, probably because they're too confusing for most people to handle. But they do exist, and it's important to know about them.

Bisexuality means that at various times a person feels emotionally, physically, and mentally attracted to both men and women. A bisexual person might date both men and women at the same time, or even have ongoing relationships with both men and women. Others may spend weeks, years, or even an entire lifetime with a person of one sex or the other, but still consider themselves bisexual.

Does this sound confusing? Well, it can be. If a woman is dating another woman, why doesn't she just say that she's a lesbian? Or if she's dating a man, why doesn't she just say that she's straight? If a man dates men for years and suddenly is attracted to a woman, does that mean that he's bisexual and not gay? These are just some of the questions that arise when discussing bisexuality.

For some people, bisexuality is a very clear thing. They are simply equally attracted to women and to men their whole lives. For others, it can be a constantly changing thing. Some men who call themselves bisexual will spend their whole lives with a woman and only have one or two relationships with men, perhaps even one or two sexual experiences with men. Or some women who identify as bisexual will have a relationship with a man and then go on to spend the rest of their lives with women. Yet all of these people may still say that they are bisexual.

The reason this gets confusing is that many people who identify as lesbian or gay do the same things. A man who says he is gay, and who has spent his entire life in relationships with men, may suddenly have a sexual experience with a woman. But he still identifies as a gay man.

A woman who identifies as a lesbian may have many sexual experiences with men, or maybe just one or two. Yet she still calls herself a lesbian. In many ways her life is exactly like the life of the woman who calls herself bisexual, but the second woman calls herself lesbian. What's the difference?

People like to be called bisexual for the same reasons that people like to be called straight, gay, lesbian, or any other name. They are proud of the fact that they find both sexes attractive, and they want people to know that, the same way I say that I am gay because I like people to know that I am attracted in many different ways to men. It is a way of identifying yourself, of letting people know who you are. Even if two people participate in the same kind of *sexual* behavior, they may choose to call themselves different things. Two men may both have other men as their primary sexual partners but also occasionally sleep with women. One man may say he's bisexual, the other may say he's gay.

This is because, like being gay or being lesbian, being bisexual isn't just about sex, even though it has the word *sexual* in its name. It's about connecting mentally, physically, and emotionally to both sexes. After all, it's not that hard to have sex with someone. Being bisexual, like being gay or being lesbian, is relating to people on many different levels. I have many women friends whom I relate to extremely well emotionally. Many of them are attractive women with whom I could theoretically have sex. But I don't relate to any of them on all of my emotional, physical, and mental levels in the same way that I relate to men. I am a gay man because when I think of the kind of person who really makes me happy physically, emotionally, and mentally, that person is another man. I could have sex with all the women in the world and it wouldn't make me bisexual, because I don't feel the same attraction to women that I do to men.

That is why people who participate in similar behavior can call themselves such different things. A woman who usually relates to other women yet sometimes relates sexually to men is still lesbian, because she finds emotional, mental, *and* sexual fulfillment in other women. Yet a woman who finds both sexes equally fulfilling on all these levels is bisexual. A man who sometimes sleeps with women yet receives his deepest, personal fulfillment from relationships with men is a gay man. Bisexual people like to be called bisexuals because that is what they are. Even if a woman is in a lifelong relationship with another woman, she might say she's bisexual and not lesbian. This is because that's what she is as a person. If she has to say she's a lesbian, then she has to ignore the fact that she could ever find the same fulfillment with a man. It may seem silly, but it's not to the person who finds herself in that position.

In a perfect world, where no one is told that they have to be one thing or another, there would probably be lots of bisexual people. This would be because we would feel free to find things attractive about people no matter what gender they were. With no rules to follow about what is "right" and what is "wrong" in terms of love and caring for one another, it would seem perfectly natural for some people to be attracted to men, some people to be attracted to women, and some people to be attracted to both. Whichever people had the qualities you find attractive would be the ones you would choose to be with. We would choose our partners based entirely on whether or not they made us happy as individuals, not on what gender they were.

Why is bisexuality an issue in the gay community? That's a sticky question, and there are many valid and invalid reasons. Many bisexual people feel that they are not welcome in the gay community. And in fact many gay people do not welcome bisexuals as part of the gay community. Why not? Again, that's complicated.

Some gay and lesbian people feel that people who call themselves bisexuals are really just gay men or lesbians who don't want to admit that they are gay. They believe that bisexual people are hiding from their true selves by pretending to be able to be attracted to both sexes so that they can be more accepted by society. Is this true? As with most things, the answer is that sometimes it is. Being gay is hard. Sometimes it's easier for people if they feel that they can somehow fit in with straight society. It's much easier for a man to say he's bisexual than to say he's gay. Why? Because, for some reason, bisexuality is often more accepted by straight people. If people can pretend that a man is "usually" straight but sometimes might be attracted to men, it is easier to accept.

Perhaps this is because it lets straight people think that the bisexual person is just "playing" when he or she has sex with someone of the same sex. Singer Elton John said for many years that he was bisexual. He even married a woman. Eventually, he came out as a gay man. When asked why he pretended to be bisexual for so long, Elton said that it made it easier for him because straight people could at least pretend that he was straight sometimes and they could ignore the gay part of him. In fact, though, he says he never was bisexual. Now he says he's very happy being gay.

This is a common story. Many people who are gay find it easier to say that they are bisexual. They date people of the opposite sex, have sex with them, and even marry them. But they continue to be attracted to people of the same sex, often more than they are attracted to the people they are married to or dating. It is very common for people who are just starting to explore their sexual feelings to say that they're bisexual. It makes them feel like they have the choice to "go back" if being gay or lesbian isn't what they want, or if it becomes too hard for them. For these people, it's much too painful to say "I'm gay," because it means that they have accepted that they are not straight. Being bisexual allows them to stay safely in the middle, and they can always go back to the straight side if they need to. This type of behavior seems to be more common among men, who feel that saying they're bisexual instead of gay means that they can still be "real" men because they sleep with women, yet they can also have sex with other men when they want to.

So all people who say they're bisexual are just in a phase, right? Well, there are some people who would like to believe that. The fact is, only we know what we are inside, what we feel and what we want. There are people who are equally attracted on all levels to both women and men, just as there are people who are attracted on all levels to either men or women. And yes, there are people who misuse the term bisexual as a way of hiding who they really are. But no one can make that decision for anyone else. People accept themselves when they are ready to, and getting angry at someone for saying that they're one thing when we think they're another is a waste of time.

Some gay and lesbian people also resent bisexuals because they feel that bisexual people only support the gay community when they are in relationships that would be considered gay by society. For example, they feel a bisexual woman will only support lesbian rights if she happens to be in a relationship with another woman. If she's in a relationship with a man, then she ignores the gay community and enjoys all of the benefits of being seen as a straight woman. But if she's with a woman, then she expects to be welcomed into the gay community as a lesbian.

This has been a problem in the gay community, but it's one that we cause by our own intolerance of bisexual people. As a rule, gay groups do not often welcome bisexual people. Because of this, many bisexual people choose not to participate in gay groups or support them, because they feel left out of the family. If they think that people will respond badly to them because they say that they're bisexual, it's easier to stay home.

Much of the animosity toward bisexual people in the gay community probably comes from fear. Just as homophobia is often caused by straight people fearing that they might have gay tendencies, many gay people see bisexual people as threatening because it makes them see possibilities other than just being gay. Is this jealousy? That's probably involved. It may also be that as gay people we spend a long time dealing with the fact that who we are is not usually accepted by straight people, and we don't like to be reminded of straight behavior because it reminds us of how we were taught we really should be, and that can be very painful.

What's interesting is that gay people who dismiss bisexuals are the same as straight people who put down gay people. We can never really know what people feel inside, or what they really think about things like who they are attracted to. It's easy for us to say that someone is pretending to be bisexual when she's really a lesbian, but we don't really know. When we say things like that, we are compartmentalizing people. Life is all about choices and opportunities. If I ever met a woman with whom I connected emotionally, physically, and sexually, I would like to think that she and I could love each other without people saying, "But you are supposed to be gay. You can't love her."

As gay people, we've been told our whole lives that we don't fit in, that being gay is not really an option for us. We have been told that we're just "in a phase" or that we're just "running from ourselves." We've spent years fighting that kind of hatred and negative thinking. Yet too often we say the same things to and about bisexuals. Are there issues about bisexuality? Yes, there are, and these need to be discussed. But bisexuals are also part of the larger gay community, because they do not fit in with the usual concepts of what people "should" be. They are part of our gay family, of our gay community, and to tell them they don't belong with us is to be just as bigoted and hateful as straight people who tell us the same thing.

The following books are good sources of information about bisexuality, as well as writings about the bisexual experience.

THE BISEXUAL ANTHOLOGY COLLECTIVE, *Plural Desires: Writing Bisexual Women's Realities* (Toronto: Sister Vision, 1995).

GARBER, MARJORIE, *Vice Versa: Bisexuality and the Eroticism of Everyday Life,* (New York: Simon & Schuster, 1994).

HUTCHINS, LORAINE AND LANI KAAHUMANU, *Bi Any Other Name: Bisexual People Speak Out* (Boston: Alyson, 1991).

KATE BORNSTEIN: PERFORMANCE ARTIST AND WRITER

"There was really no talk about gender in my home," says writer and performer Kate Bornstein. "We didn't really think of ourselves as having gender. There was Mom and Dad and my brother and me. That was it. Gender was something that happened to me when I went to nursery school [when I was] four and a half and they split us up into boys' lines and girls' lines. This was really surprising to me. I looked at the boys' line and what they were doing there, and it didn't look right to me. And I looked over at the girls' line, and that looked a lot more appealing. So I went over there. I knew I was a boy, but I'd never really been asked to put myself into that box before. So I figured I must be a little girl. I really figured that. It wasn't that I thought I was a boy who was pretending to be a girl. I really thought that I must be a little girl and that my parents must have made a mistake. And the teacher looked at me with this horrible look and ordered me into the boys' line. I worked for a long time—the next fifteen years really—on trying to fit into the boys' line."

Today, Kate draws on those memories, as well as on her subsequent experiences as a transsexual person, to create thoughtful, entertaining, and often controversial work dealing with how gender affects the way people see themselves and see others. Her book *Gender Outlaw: On Men, Women, and the Rest of Us* describes her own experiences and encounters with the limits of sexual expectations, and for audiences across the country she has performed her solo performance pieces *The Opposite Sex Is Neither* and *Virtually Yours: A Game for Solo Performer with Audience.*

Kate says she knew from a very early age that her physical gender did not match what she was feeling inside. While not much was available about the subject, she sought information about people like herself, and found it in the person of Christine Jorgensen, the first transsexual person to draw national attention. "I thought of being transsexual as an option from the time I was eleven years old, because that's when Christine Jorgensen came out as transsexual," she recalls. "She was dragged out of the closet and raked through the *National Enquirer.* I bought every issue, religiously looking for more about her and folks like me. Only it really scared the hell out of me when I read what you had to do. You had to go all the way to Denmark. You had to have this painful surgery. You had to have hormones. It was scary. I had no idea what they were talking about, and I didn't want to be one of those people if that's what I had to do."

As she grew older, Kate struggled with trying to fit her emotions and feelings into the "correct" box. Attracted to women, she had no way to define her feelings. "I thought that I must be gay," she says, "because I thought that if I was really a female, then I had to love men, because that's what women did. And I did have relationships with men. But I really had this thing for women, and so that confused me even more. I was bisexual, that's for sure, but we didn't have that word then."

After a long process of self-discovery, Kate did come out as a transsexual person. What she found, though, was that, just like the straight community, the gay community also had preconceived ideas about gender identity. "When I first came out, I ran to the gay and lesbian community thinking, 'Oh, God, I'm finally home,'" she says. "And I was met with a lot of acceptance, but also enough suspicion and anger to make me scared, to make me cry. And that still happens sometimes. There are still places where I can't go, where I am not welcome."

Still, she believes that the gay community is beginning to recognize that there are many different ways to express sexuality and gender. Discussing the changing nature of what used to be called simply "the gay and lesbian community," Kate says, "I like the word *queer* because it includes us all. The way I look at it, I'm not part of the gay community. That's a community that I can walk through, and I certainly have lots of friends who are part of it. But I don't think I am part of it. I think I am part of a larger community that includes the gay community, a community I would call a queer community or an outlaw community or a transgendered community. These are people who break rules of gender. There are lots of ways that people break gender, and I am part of a family of people who break gender rules."

While many women and men do undergo transsexual surgery, Kate points out that there are many different options available now to people who want to experiment with their genders. "I would encourage anyone who is thinking about this subject to look in other directions, to find people who are playing with gender, who are trying different ways of expressing gender. If you want to put on different types of clothing, do it. And if it is the clothes you like, have a good time. These are just not things we are told about. But the options do exist. You aren't crazy. There are people like us. If someone is reading this and thinks, 'Well, maybe I'm not a girl' or 'Maybe I'm not a boy,' well, it's something to put in your back pocket and think about. There are many, many options available to people now. Just because you decide you're not a boy, it doesn't mean you have to go cut off your penis. Be a girl with a penis. If you were assigned the label 'girl,' and you don't think it's right, it doesn't have to mean you're a guy. And if you're a butch girl, it doesn't always mean you're a lesbian. It just means you're butch. These are the things I've learned, that you can be all of these different things. And I know this isn't easy for people to understand, or even follow, but for those who do, it can be a wonderful relief."

While many people, including gay and lesbian people, find it hard to understand the concept of living as a gender different from what their bodies say they are, or what others see them as, Kate believes that most of us are breaking rules of gender, even when we don't always know it. "The only gender, the only identity, that's safe in this world, to some degree as an illusion of safety, is white, heterosexual, able-bodied, middle-class, middle-aged, Christian, Anglo-Saxon male," she says. "Anything that falls away from that in any degree is less safe. You take away 'white' and you're less safe. You take away

'Christian' and you're less safe. You take away 'able-bodied' and you're less safe. So as queer people, or as women, or as anything different from that definition, we are living dangerous lives. We are living in ways that are not considered safe."

The experience of living as a transgendered person has taught Kate a lot about herself and about people, even when it has not been easy. "It is painful, and it is lonely. And sometimes I still do cry," she says. "But I am a lot happier since I did this than I ever was wondering if I should. In the movies, you always see people who are outsiders. And the more they stand up for themselves, even though they have to go through a lot of pain and suffering, in the end they end up with better friends. And I think that's what's happening to me in this part of my life. As much as I would love to wave a little wand and make everybody understand, people are going to have to learn this for themselves. That's the biggest lesson of going through this for me."

Her advice to anyone who feels out of place, for any reason, is to understand that they are not alone. "I would say to anyone who thinks she or he is a freak, for whatever reason, stick with it. Love it. Love that about yourself. There will be times when you want to run away from it. Run away for a little while, but always come back. Don't be afraid of who or what you are. And keep looking, because there are going to be people who accept you for what you are. And they're worth waiting for. It's worth fighting for."

GENDER MATTERS

Like bisexuals, another group of people in the gay community who are often overlooked or even hidden are *transsexuals* and *transgendered people,* those who feel that their physical genders do not match the genders they relate to emotionally and mentally. The prefix *trans-* means "transfer," so a transgendered person is someone whose gender has been switched in some way. These people may feel that they are "trapped" inside bodies that do not reflect their true selves.

A transsexual person is a person who physically alters her or his sex from one to the other. Transsexual people have had surgery to make their outer selves correspond to their inner selves. While transsexual people are transgendered people, not all people who are transgendered have had surgery, so they aren't all transsexual.

Like bisexuals, transgendered people are increasingly visible and vocal members of the gay community. Unfortunately, they are also some of the most misunderstood people in the gay world. Many people confuse transgendered people with *transvestites*—people who enjoy dressing up as the opposite sex, usually just because it's fun for them. They do not think that they're the opposite sex, nor do they usually want to be the opposite sex. They just like dressing up. The term is usually applied to men who like to dress up as women, but there are also many women who enjoy dressing as men. Many transvestites are actually straight men who just enjoy dressing in women's clothing because it excites them or because it's fun. But there are a number of gay men who also enjoy dressing as women. Men who dress as women are also called "drag queens." Women who dress as men are called "drag kings."

It is very important to understand that *transgendered* people are not people who just decide they want to be something else because it sounds interesting. Nor are they merely effeminate men who look and act like women and who "might as well be women" or big, masculine women who act like men and "might as well be men." They are people who very much feel that there is a difference between the ways their physical bodies look and the ways their mental, spiritual, and emotional selves relate to those bodies. While transsexuals get enjoyment out of pretending to be the opposite sex, for transgendered people the experience of knowing that their physical sexes don't match their emotional ones can often be very painful and not at all enjoyable.

Another misconception about transgendered people is that they are just lesbian or gay people who want to be the opposite sex because they can't deal with being gay. This also is not true. Some males who become females do have relationships with men. But just as many form lesbian relationships with other women. Similarly, females who become males are just as likely to form gay relationships with other men as they are to form relationships with women. All of our notions about straight, gay, and lesbian, and about what is male and what is female become tossed around in new ways.

This can be very hard for those of us who have not been through it to understand. You might even feel frightened or disgusted by the thought of people believing that they should be the opposite sex or of people "changing" their sex from one thing to another. You might think, as many people do, that transgendered people are just confused about who they are. Or you might think they should just learn to live with the bodies they have. But it isn't that simple, and if you know more about the subject, it can help you understand what is being talked about.

One theory about transgendered people is that they simply got the wrong bodies at birth. When a group of cells begins to form into a human being after fertilization, a number of things happen. One of the things that happens is that sexual organs form. What's very interesting is that female and male genitals both form from the same group of cells. What becomes the penis in a male becomes a clitoris in a female. The clitoris is a sexual organ inside a woman's vagina. It looks very much like a tiny penis, and is similar in that it is extremely sensitive and is capable of great sexual pleasure. Similarly, what forms into the scrotum and testicles in a male becomes the vagina and ovaries in a female.

After these organs form, the body begins to secrete hormones specific to the sex determined by the sex organs. For example, if the cells form testicles, then the body begins to secrete the hormone testosterone, which gives men more body hair, deeper voices, and different muscle builds than women have. It also affects some personality traits, like aggression. If the cells form a vagina and ovaries, the body begins to secrete a female hormone, estrogen, which is what causes breasts to form and the menstrual cycle to start, and it affects things like voice range and body shape. In essence, our bodies begin to form around the kind of genitals we have. Sometimes, however, as a person develops he or she starts to feel that something isn't quite right. A young woman may feel she just isn't supposed to have the breasts that are suddenly developing. Or a young man might feel the penis between his legs is out of place. This may sound funny, but it can be horribly confusing and frightening. People who feel that their bodies are somehow "wrong" may think that they're going crazy. They may feel shameful, depressed, or even suicidal.

This is only one theory of why some people are transgendered. There are certainly others, some of them focusing on biology and some of them on psychology theories. What it comes down to, though, is all about how we see gender. We are taught that certain things are male and that certain things are female, that men behave in certain ways and women behave in certain ways that are different from how men behave. Some languages, like French, even designate words as being either masculine or feminine depending on how they are perceived. Basically, we have a long list of things that mean female and a long list of things that mean male. If you have a penis between your legs, you are supposed to act in the ways that men are expected to act. If you have a vagina, you are supposed to act in the ways that women are expected to act. This is because we have very set ideas of how each gender behaves.

Transgendered people do not act or behave or think in the ways that society has said that they should based on what kind of physical genders they have. A transgendered man may grow up wanting to wear dresses, have a high voice, put on makeup, and many other things associated with being female. He may act in ways considered feminine. He doesn't want to do these things because they're different; he just feels that that's what he should do. A transgendered woman may grow up wanting to have a beard, wear suits, and talk in a deep voice. She may even look very masculine and act in ways considered masculine. This is just how she feels.

Many of us do things that are considered "wrong" for our sex. I grew up knowing how to sew and cook. Many women grow up playing baseball and fishing, things traditionally considered masculine. This doesn't mean we are transgendered. Just being interested in things usually associated with the opposite sex doesn't make you transgendered. Being transgendered means knowing deep inside you that somehow something is just not right about the way you feel you should be and the way you are expected to be because of your physical gender. It is a strong, deep knowledge that you feel in every part of yourself.

How transgendered people deal with this difference between their bodies and minds varies. Some simply choose to live their lives dressing and behaving as though they are the genders they are inside. They go by names associated with the opposite gender, use rest rooms of the opposite gender, wear clothing of the opposite gender, and act and appear in nearly every way as the gender they are inside.

For years there were no other options for people who were transgendered, and many people, especially women, lived their lives the only way they knew how, simply by acting as the gender they felt they were. Many transgendered women dressed as men, got work as men, and lived completely as men. This was harder for men to do, because physically it is harder for men to pass as women. But some did do it. It was often illegal for people to behave or dress as the opposite sex, and many women and men who did were routinely abused by the police or arrested for being criminals. And often both transgendered women and men were beaten or killed when their "secrets" were discovered.

Some transgendered people do choose to alter their bodies physically to match the gender they feel they are. They have operations (actually a long series of operations) in which their bodies are made to match the genders they feel inside. This is called *gender reassignment*, what is commonly but mistakenly called sex-change operations. Transsexual people do not feel they are changing from one sex to another, which implies that they are choosing to become something else. They feel they already are something else and are simply fixing their physical bodies to match their true identities.

Gender reassignment is a very long and demanding process that can take many years to complete. It is emotionally and financially very difficult. Insurance plans do not cover gender reassignment surgery, so people who want to go through it have to pay for it themselves. And because the whole area of gender reassignment has not been studied extensively, women and men who choose to undergo the procedure experience enormous pressure in dealing with friends, coworkers, family, and practically everyone they come into contact with on a day-to-day basis. Transsexual people frequently encounter fear, discrimination, and hatred when they tell people what they are doing, and many have had to begin their lives all over again after gender reassignment.

In many cases, especially in male-to-female transgendered people (female-to-male is still very difficult), you cannot even tell that a person has had gender reassignment surgery. Transgendered people work as fashion models, actors, teachers, firefighters, and anything else you can think of. One male-to-female person was a highly paid model and actress who posed nude for *Playboy* magazine before anyone knew she had once been male. But despite increasing success with surgeries and greater visibility in the gay community, transgendered people still have a very hard time. No matter what a person looks like on the outside, when people find out that someone has changed his or her gender all kinds of thoughts and feelings go through their heads. Many people, and this includes people in the gay community, feel that transgendered people aren't "real" women or "real" men because they haven't lived their whole lives having to face and deal with what a person born female or born male does.

This may be true, but transgendered people have gone through just as tough, and maybe tougher, a struggle than the rest of us. They have had to go through the process of examining who they are and what they are on the inside. They have dealt with feeling trapped in a body that doesn't reflect who they are as people. Even after surgery they have to live with other people's judgments and prejudices. More than most of us, they have come to understand what it means to be not only men or women, but human beings.

This process can be especially hard for young people who feel that something just isn't right between their bodies and their emotions and who often have no idea what is going on. Just as we aren't usually taught that being lesbian, bisexual, or gay is a valid way to live, we certainly aren't taught that we might have bodies that don't fit who we really are. Often transgendered young people think they're just crazy, that something is wrong with their minds. With no one to talk to, they can become confused, unhappy, and suicidal.

Teena Brandon was a young woman who believed that she should have been born male. She looked male, she acted male, she dressed in men's clothing, and she thought of herself as male. She lived in the small town of Falls City, Nebraska, where she called herself Brandon Teena and lived as a man. I will call her Brandon because that is what she chose to be called. Brandon also preferred to be called "he," but I will use the word "she" because it is less confusing. Brandon had many girlfriends and was very popular as a kind and generous man; that is, until someone discovered that the person they thought was a male was really female.

In late 1993, Brandon was forced by a group of men who had heard that she might not be male to undress in front of a crowd of people at a party. She was then raped and beaten. When she reported the incident to the local police, they did nothing about it, implying that she had brought the incident on herself by trying to "trick" people. A week later, two of the men who raped Brandon came to her house again. This time they beat her again. They also shot her and two friends execution-style, killing all three. The men did this because they thought it was disgusting for a person to "fool" them that way. Brandon Teena was twenty-one years old. In 1995, John Lotter and Marvin Thomas Nissen were tried and convicted for the three murders.

We will never know what Brandon Teena's life would be like had she lived. We do know that she thought of herself as male and that others thought of her as male. She lived as a male. Many newspaper accounts of the story referred to Brandon as "he" out of respect for her image of herself. Some people say that Brandon Teena was not a transgendered person because all she did was wear men's clothes and "act like a man." They say she was a transvestite.

Was Brandon Teena a transgendered person? Probably she was. Had more resources and information been available to her, she might have called herself transgendered. She might even have taken steps toward changing her outer body to fit her inner person. But we'll never know what her choice would have been. Two people filled with hate over something they didn't understand—John Lotter and Marvin Thomas Nissen—took all of her rights away from her when they killed her.

If you are a young person who has thought that maybe there is something different about the way your body and your inner self go together, you aren't crazy or sick or abnormal. Many transgendered people felt something was "different" at a very young age. This doesn't mean that every person who feels uncomfortable with her or his body is transgendered. All of us feel uncomfortable with ourselves at some time. But some of you might be transgendered, and it's important for you to know that there are people available who understand what you're going through and can help you. The resource section at the back of this book lists organizations that offer assistance to young people seeking information on transgendered issues. There are also many good books and magazines about transgender issues, and these are also listed.

For those of us who are not transgendered, it is important for us to learn more about people who are. You probably think you will never know someone who is transgendered. I know that's what I thought. I thought the only place I would ever see transgendered people was on television talk shows. But now one of the dearest people in my life is a transgendered person. She is a good friend, and I respect her enormously. She is one of the kindest, bravest people I know, and a talented writer and performer. She has taught me many things about how I look at gender and helped me to get rid of many of the misconceptions and stereotypes I had about people.

Just as the gay community is often not accepting of bisexual people, we often overlook transgendered people. Many lesbian organizations shut out transgendered women because they weren't born biological women. Many gay groups say that if a person born male becomes a female who says she is a lesbian, that the person isn't really lesbian because she wasn't born a woman. The arguments can get very stupid and very heated. The point is that people are what they say they are, not what we say they are. Transgendered people are gay people, and they are part of the gay community. As members of the gay community, it is up to us to accept them just as we expect to be accepted.

Unfortunately, few solid books about transgendered people are available. The good news is that the ones that are available are excellent.

BORNSTEIN, KATE, *Gender Matters: On Men, Women, and the Rest of Us* (New York: Routledge, 1994).

DEVOR, HOLLY, *Gender Blending: Confronting the Limits of Duality* (Indianapolis, IN: Indiana University Press, 1989).

MORRIS, JAN, *Conundrum: An Extraordinary Narrative of Transsexualism* (New York: Henry Holt, 1984). This is a fascinating biography of one of the first transsexual people to make her story public.

GAY STUDIES 101: EDUCATIONAL OPPORTUNITIES

For many gay people, going away to college is one of the most exciting times in our lives. It's usually the first time we are away from our families and living on our own. We are able to make some of our own decisions and choose what we are going to do. For many of us, it's the first time we are able to begin exploring our gay identities. For some, it's even the first time we realize that we are gay.

Gay issues are also taking on increasing importance at colleges and universities. As more gay women and men come out as young people, they are looking for schools that will give them good educations but will also offer them chances to explore their sexualities and to learn about gay issues in their classes. Some students even want to major in gay and lesbian studies.

Today, many schools around the country are providing services for gay students. Some provide counseling for gay students to help them come out, along with sponsoring gay social and support groups. Some teach classes in lesbian and gay history, literature, politics, and social issues. A few even provide housing for gay couples and have gay and lesbian fraternities and sororities. If you are thinking about school or are already in school, you may be looking for ways to make your gay identity a greater part of your educational experience. You may just want to attend a school where you can be open about being gay, or you may want to attend a school that offers classes in gay issues.

Many colleges today have some kind of gay student group. These groups may be part of the school's student activities union, or they may be informal. If you are looking at school catalogs and don't see anything about lesbian and gay students, it doesn't necessarily mean there isn't a group on campus or that there are no gay students. Many colleges play down the presence of gay student groups out of fear of offending parents. The best way to find out if a school is someplace you want to be as a gay student is to visit the campus and ask around. Chances are, you'll find out there's a gay group somewhere.

A useful book for gay people thinking about school is *The Gay, Lesbian, and Bisexual Students' Guide to Colleges, Universities, and Graduate Schools.* Compiled from questionnaires sent out to colleges around the country, the book gives descriptions of many different schools based on what gay students who attend those schools have to say. The descriptions include students' opinions of gay classes, what it's like to be gay on campus, what social activities are available to gay students, and what the school's policy is toward gay people.

The book does not cover all the schools in the country, or even most of them, and it doesn't include any information about costs of attending the schools or other practical information. What it does do is give you the opinions of other students who attend the schools, which can be very helpful if you have no other way of visiting the school or if you just want to see what other people think. Reading what other gay people have to say about a certain school may help you decide if it's a place you would think about going.

Obviously, schools in larger cities like New York, Chicago, or San Francisco are going to have larger gay student groups than, say, a college in a small city in Ohio. But don't think you have to go to a big-city school to find a gay community. Many smaller schools and schools in less populated areas also have such groups. Even a local community college probably has some kind of group, even if it's a little harder to find. So, if going away to a larger city isn't an option for you, don't despair. With a little searching, you'll probably find the school you attend has a number of gay students.

10 COLLEGES AND UNIVERSITIES POPULAR WITH GAY STUDENTS

1. **SMITH COLLEGE,** Northampton, MA

2. **COLUMBIA UNIVERSITY,** New York, NY

3. **AMERICAN UNIVERSITY,** Washington, D.C.

4. **BRANDEIS UNIVERSITY,** Waltham, MA

5. **BROWN UNIVERSITY,** Providence, RI

6. **CITY UNIVERSITY OF NEW YORK,** New York, NY

7. **HAMPSHIRE COLLEGE,** Amherst, MA

8. **NEW YORK UNIVERSITY,** New York, NY

9. **OBERLIN COLLEGE,** Oberlin, OH

10. **UNIVERSITY OF NORTH CAROLINA,** Chapel Hill, NC

If you are just beginning to think about going to college, you might also want to think about ways in which you can use your college experience to become more involved in the gay community, both socially and professionally. Joining a gay group at school is a great way to meet other gay people. Beyond that, it may offer you the opportunity to become involved in some political issues, such as working to get antidiscrimination policy implemented at your school or perhaps to get AIDS education and condom programs in use. These experiences will be invaluable later if you decide to become involved in gay issues after you graduate.

On a larger scale, you may want to use your time at school to think about how you would like to be involved in the gay community after you graduate. For example, perhaps you are interested in becoming a lawyer. You might think about using your law skills to help the gay community, and take some classes that focus on public policy or human rights law. If you want to become a doctor, maybe you'd like to include some study of women's health issues in your program so that later you can work with lesbian health concerns. If social services is your field, you may be able to use what you learn to aid gay young people.

Even courses that may not seem to have anything to do with gay people can be helpful in planning your future as a part of the gay community. If you major in history, try to find out what roles gay people played in history. If English is your field, you have many different opportunities to study the contributions of gay women and men to literature. Even physical education majors can orient their studies toward working in the gay community. Thinking ahead to how you can use your skills later in life can help you plan how you might be involved in the gay community.

College can be a wonderful time for exploring who you are as a gay person. It's a time when you can meet other people and see what kinds of things are available to you as a gay man or woman. If your school is located near an active gay community, you have many opportunities to join different kinds of groups and, maybe for the first time, to meet other openly gay people or people who are different from you in some way. Perhaps being away from home and some of the pressures that creates will allow you to try new things and become involved in things you might not have thought about before.

Even if you've already been through school, further education can be a wonderful way to get yourself involved in the community. Many men and women find that going back for another degree or a higher degree in their chosen field leads them into interesting possibilities for becoming more involved in the gay community. For example, a friend of mine with a degree in social services decided that she wanted to become more involved in the gay community. After going back to school for her master's degree, she started a practice counseling lesbian and gay people. Another friend, a businessman, went back to school for his MBA degree and then started a financial planning service for gay people. He also volunteers with an AIDS organization, offering his financial skills to help them form budgets and get donations.

Whatever stage of education you're at, you can use what you learn to expand your knowledge of gay issues and to become more involved in the gay community. This could be as simple as choosing a college with an active gay students' organization, or as involved as going back to school to study gay rights issues and then joining a law firm fighting for gay rights. How involved you choose to get is up to you.

BOSTON, MASSACHUSETTS — Sarah Grant

What's it like to be gay, lesbian, bisexual, or transgendered in Boston? Exciting, scary, intellectually stimulating, frustrating, affirming, welcoming, lonely, enriching, challenging. In other words, not so different from what it might be like in many other cities, but also uniquely different. Boston has a rich queer past. It was the site of nineteenth-century "Boston marriages"—committed, long-term, live-in relationships between two women. It elected the country's first openly gay person to a state legislature (Elaine Noble in 1974). Massachusetts congresspersons Gerry Studds and Barney Frank were the first two members of Congress to come out of the closet. Since then, both have been repeatedly reelected. The first gay Asian group in the nation (BAGMAL) was founded here in 1979. Cambridge, home of Harvard College, currently boasts the first openly gay African-American mayor in the nation, Ken Reeves. Massachusetts was the second state in the nation to pass a gay rights bill (1989) and the first in the nation to pass a bill of rights for lesbian and gay students. There's obviously a large, politically active lesbian and gay community here.

Several things make Boston a unique place for gay women and men to live. For one thing, it's a city that loves sports. And the queer community is no exception. Organized gay teams exist for almost any sport you can think of: swimming, volleyball, basketball, bowling, and so on. In fact, Boston's lesbian softball league, with twenty-two teams, is the largest in the nation.

Culture and the arts of all kinds are also important to the residents of Boston, and the lesbian and gay community supports many different kinds of artistic events. Boston is home to many bands playing all kinds of music, and queer musicians including Tracy Chapman, Patty Larkin, and Katie Curtis are just a few of the performers to come out of Boston's gay music scene. In addition, Boston is a very literary city. Queer writers thrive here, and many opportunities exist for writers of all kinds to share their work. All of the city's gay and lesbian bookstores hold regular public readings, and many writers' groups exist to offer critiques and support. The queer writing event of the year—the annual lesbian and gay writers' conference called OutWrite—takes place annually in Boston.

Another great thing about Boston's gay community is the unusually high degree of interaction and cooperation between gay men and lesbians. Unlike many other cities, where the two groups seldom work together, in Boston men and women are often found playing and working together.

So how can you find your place in Boston's queer community? One of the easiest ways is to move to one of the lesbian or gay neighborhoods in the city. Jamaica Plain (J.P.), a community just a couple of miles from downtown Boston, is fondly and proudly known as the "Lesbian Nation" because of the high concentration of lesbians who live there. A number of gay men are also finding J.P. a great place to live. J.P. is the most racially, ethnically, and economically integrated neighborhood in the Boston area, and this alone wins over the hearts of many people. Home to many artists and writers (both gay and straight), it boasts one of the city's two women's bookstores, Crone's Harvest (the other is New Words in Cambridge). J.P. is rife with coffee shops, eateries, and funky businesses. Two of the easiest ways to meet other people in J.P. are to get a dog and take it for a walk or to stop into J.P. Licks, the local gourmet ice cream shop. Either way, you can't help rubbing shoulders with other wonderful folks, especially women.

For gay men, the neighborhood of choice is the South End. Situated right in the city, the South End is home to the largest concentration of gay men in Boston. Rainbow flags are everywhere. There are restaurants galore in the neighborhood, and most are gay-owned and operated. One of the city's two exclusively gay and lesbian bookstores, We Think the World of You, is located here. The other, Glad Day Bookstore, is only blocks away. Both bookstores are good places to check out, as they have active and interesting bulletin boards with information on everything from finding a roommate to upcoming cultural events. The South End is also the home of the Theatre Offensive, the city's queer theater venue. The theater hosts a yearly performance festival titled "Out on the Edge," in addition to sponsoring smaller events throughout the year.

If you're a person who wants to live in a very gay-friendly neighborhood but one where you are not in the majority, the areas of Cambridge and Somerville are both good choices. Wherever you choose to live, the odds are that you'll find a neighborhood social group made up of the other lesbian, gay, and bisexual people there. Few communities in the Boston area are without them.

Although Boston does not have an official gay community center, there are two places that go a long way toward filling this gap. The first is the Fenway Community Health Center (617-267-0900), located close to downtown. It provides health care, mental health services, AIDS care and education, a victim recovery assistance program, and support groups for many different types of people, including women having children through artificial insemination, Latina lesbians, men of color, gay and lesbian parents, and women and men dealing with issues about HIV/AIDS.

The second surrogate community center is located at 29 Stanhope Street in the South End. This building houses a myriad of queer and HIV service groups and nonprofit organizations. The Names Project (an AIDS memorial group), Dignity (a gay Catholics group), The Speakers' Bureau, BSEF (which publishes *Gay Community News* and organizes the OutWrite conference and the Gay & Lesbian Prisoners' Project), the Boston Living Center (HIV support services including alternative therapies, meals, and support groups), and others all have offices here. Both Fenway and 29 Stanhope are great places to become involved in volunteer activities that support the lesbian and gay community and to connect with other people who may have similar interests and experiences.

Queers in Boston are involved in every level of politics. Lesbians and gay men fill a number of high-profile political positions in the city and the state, and gay political action groups, lobbyists, and alliances are extremely active. Are you Republican? Try joining the Log Cabin Republican Club. Are you an in-your-face dyke? Then join the fire-swallowing Lesbian Avengers. Are you committed to the rights of gay women and men to marry? Then you might want to hook up with the Forum on the Right to Marriage. Or maybe you're a guerilla art activist. Check out Wake Up, a group that combats stereotypes and discrimination through art actions.

There are many other good ways to find the gay, lesbian, bisexual, and transgendered community in Boston. One is to join the rest of queer Boston for Pride Weekend in early June. The highlight of Pride is the parade and celebration on Saturday, for which 100,000 people turned out in 1995. The first annual Dyke March joined the Pride festivities in 1995, initiated by lesbians who felt that the parade had lost its political character.

Being lesbian or gay doesn't mean that you have to give up your spirituality or your religion, and Boston's gay community has much to offer queer people looking for places to worship. The Metropolitan Community Church (nondenominational), Am Tikva (Jewish), and Dignity (Catholic) all hold regular services. The Arlington Street Church, a church located in downtown Boston, is led by Minister Kim Crawford Harvie, an out lesbian. Not surprisingly, most of her congregation is lesbian, gay, and bisexual. A fair number of straight churches in Boston also reach out to the gay community and welcome gay people.

For gay young adults, Boston offers several ways to become acquainted with the queer community. Gay and Lesbian Adolescent Social Services (GLASS) (617-266-3349) offers workshops, support groups, job training, theater and creative arts classes, as well as a drop-in center. Proud, Inc. (617-43-PROUD), sponsors Boston Area Gay and Lesbian Youth (BAGLY) and Healthy, Strong, and Proud (HSP).

BAGLY (800-42-BAGLY) holds social events and twice weekly discussions and support meetings for queer women and men between the ages of sixteen and twenty-two. HSP is a peer-led HIV/AIDS information and prevention service.

If you are a transgendered person, there are a number of places for you to get connected to the queer community. You might start with the International Foundation for Gender Education (IFGE) (617-899-8340), an educational, advocacy, and referral center. The Tiffany Club of New England hosts social events, runs support groups, and staffs a hotline (617-891-9325). Most of their members are cross-dressers. For female-to-male transgendered persons, you can contact Enterprise, a weekly support group, by calling at 617-983-3264.

Another advantage to living in Boston is that when you get that irresistible urge to get out of town for the weekend, you don't have to leave the queer world behind you. Just a couple of hours' drive from Boston are two other gay meccas—Provincetown on Cape Cod and Northampton in western Massachusetts. Both are beautiful places to go for a relaxing weekend or a vacation. Boston is also only a few hours away by plane, bus, train, or car from New York and other cities.

There are as many ways to be queer in Boston as there are kinds of queer people. As you go about finding and making your own niche, remember to start with what you already know about yourself. Whatever your interests or background, you're sure to find other queers who enjoy sharing the same things you do.

SARAH GRANT is a queer dyke who has lived in Boston for ten years. She is the Administrative Director of the Bromfield Street Educational Foundation and the coordinator of the annual OutWrite conference.

LIVING AND WORKING

Once gay people flocked to cities because they really were the only places to be gay and out. The sheer size of cities offered anonymity and protection to women and men who couldn't be out as lesbians and gay men in smaller towns. Cities like New York and San Francisco had thriving gay communities long before people heard of gay liberation or gay rights. The cities also provided many employment opportunities not available in rural areas.

Cities are still great places for gay people to live. Many cities have neighborhoods that are largely gay or areas with lots of gay stores, bars, and restaurants. And cities offer access to wonderful things such as museums, theaters, galleries, concerts, ballet, sporting events, and other cultural attractions. Many gay women and men enjoy cities because they provide a strong, visible gay community that makes it easier to be a gay person.

But cities are not the only option. Today, more and more gay people are moving away from big cities into smaller cities and towns. It is not uncommon to find gay people in even the smallest towns across the United States.

This isn't to say that it's always easy to be a gay person everywhere in America. In fact, there are some cities in which anti-gay forces are trying to pass laws that would prevent us from living there happily. In Oregon, for example, there is a long-running campaign to prevent gay people from having equal rights and to make it illegal even to discuss homosexuality in public schools. Several other states, including Maine and Florida, have also faced similar campaigns. While none of these campaigns has been ultimately successful, they have been actively supported by many people who feel that gay people should not be allowed to live freely in their cities.

When you are thinking about where you would like to live, you might want to take into consideration what life is like in that place for gay people. For example, are there local laws that make discrimination against gay people illegal? There are currently no national laws about such issues, so it is up to states and local governments to pass such legislation. Why are these types of laws important? Without them, it may be possible for someone to refuse to rent you an apartment or a house because you are gay. Someone may refuse to give you a job because you are gay. It may even be possible for someone to harass you because you are gay and not have to face any punishment.

Another important factor when choosing a place to live is what kind of community you want to be in. Some cities have very active gay communities; others have small, unorganized communities. If you are a person who wants to be actively involved in gay politics or social issues, then it might be better for you to be in a city like Atlanta or Los Angeles than in a small town or out in the country. If you like quiet surroundings, then you probably won't be happy in someplace like New York.

Some places are particularly known for having gay communities. Northampton, Massachusetts, for example, is often called the Lesbian Capital of the World because so many lesbians live there. And obviously metropolitan areas like Washington, D.C., or Minneapolis, Minnesota, are going to have more gay people than a ranching community in Wyoming or a tiny Maine fishing town. But wherever you might want to go, you can. You don't have to move somewhere just because you want to be part of a gay community. The gay community is in every type of city imaginable, from a busy place like New York to a more relaxed one like Seattle, Washington.

Just as we can live wherever we want to as gay people, we can also hold any kind of job we want to. As you've seen from the profiles in this book, lesbian and gay people come from all walks of life. Sometimes we don't think about this. We're used to thinking that being gay narrows the opportunities available to us, and think that we can have only certain jobs or be in certain professions. This is because for many years people assumed that gay people held only certain jobs, like hairdressers or airline stewards.

Well, some of us are hairdressers and airline stewards. But we are also movie directors, carpenters, kindergarten teachers, scientists, lawyers, army officers, gardeners, stockbrokers, and artists. And while there is still discrimination against gay people, this hasn't stopped gay women and men from becoming CEOs or successes in their chosen fields.

Because gay issues are becoming increasingly important, and because companies are beginning to recognize that gay employees are key parts of their successes, many businesses have begun to address the concerns of gay employees. A number of companies have added gay antidiscrimination policies, making it illegal for someone to be fired because she is a lesbian or not hired because he is gay. Some companies have very active gay employee groups that hold social functions and monitor the company's response to gay issues. Companies are also offering health benefits to the partners of gay employees.

Again, this doesn't mean that it's always easy to be a gay person in every field. Even though many

10 COMPANIES CONSIDERED POSITIVE PLACES FOR GAY EMPLOYEES TO WORK

1. BEN & JERRY'S

2. THE WALT DISNEY COMPANY

3. LEVI STRAUSS & CO.

4. STARBUCKS COFFEE CO.

5. APPLE COMPUTER INC.

6. SCHOLASTIC INC.

7. NATIONAL PUBLIC RADIO

8. CELESTIAL SEASONINGS, INC.

9. HARLEY DAVIDSON, INC.

10. GREENPEACE INTERNATIONAL

police departments actively recruit lesbian and gay officers, that doesn't mean gay officers always have an easy time being out. Gay teachers have frequently come under attack for discussing gay issues in class, and the military still makes life very difficult for gay soldiers. There are always going to be people who simply are afraid of gay people and want to give us a hard time. But despite the problems that remain, gay people have the opportunity to be whatever we want to be.

If you are thinking ahead to what you might want to do as a career, you may want to consider how companies or organizations you are interested in working for address gay issues. Will your partner, if you have one, be eligible for health benefits? Does the company support any gay organizations, or will they match any donations you make to a gay organization? Or does the company support any anti-gay organizations or causes? Are there other gay people in the company, and how do they feel about working there?

Obviously some of these questions you can answer only after working someplace for a while. But others you can find out about easily just by asking the company recruiter or head of personnel. There are also some books about gay people in the workplace, including *The 100 Best Companies for Gay Men and Lesbians* by Ed Mickens. This book lists both large and small companies that are considered great places for gay people to work based on how the companies address gay issues and how other gay people who work there feel about the companies. Books like this one can be both interesting and helpful for people looking for more information about possible job opportunities.

Aside from mainstream employers, there are many businesses that have simply refocused their skills to meet the needs of the gay community. For example, a number of doctors have opened gay-specific practices focusing on the health needs of gay women and men. Some law firms handle only gay issues. There are gay caterers, movers, decorating firms, publishers, architectural firms, and many other kinds of businesses specifically serving the gay community. There are also political organizations such as the National Gay and Lesbian Task Force (NGLTF), the Gay and Lesbian Alliance Against Defamation (GLAAD), and the Human Rights Campaign Fund (HRCF) that work nationally on lesbian and gay issues.

These kinds of businesses and organizations can be great places to work because they involve you directly with the gay community and offer a way for you to use your skills and interests to affect the gay community positively. You can also be out at work and be around other gay people most of the time.

Some gay people have also chosen to make their gay identities an integral part of their work lives by creating their own jobs or businesses centered around being gay. A lot of women and men have created very successful businesses simply by looking around at the gay community and thinking of something that gay people might buy or need.

Creating your own business can be exciting. It can also be a great way for you to create a job for yourself and maybe even for other people where you use your skills and interests in a way that you enjoy. It also allows you to become more involved with the gay community. Gay people tend to support gay-owned businesses, and many business owners find being involved with the community to be a very positive experience.

Many gay people are happy working in the straight community or in jobs not related to the gay community at all. But many are also happy matching their career choices with their gay lives. Whatever you want to do, you should know that you can. How much being a gay person influences your choice is entirely up to you.

ANDY MANGELS: COMIC BOOK WRITER AND EDITOR

"As a kid growing up in Big Fork, Montana, I had very few friends," recalls Andy Mangels. "Because of that, I read a lot and retreated a lot into worlds of fantasy. One of the neatest places for that was comic books, because it provided me with something visual and something written at the same time. That led me to creating my own adventures in my mind. I had an active imagination, and when I was doing things in my mind, it was always creating something similar to what I saw in comic books. So I grew up wanting to work in the comic book field somehow."

Andy pursued his dream of working in the comic industry, and today he is a respected comic book writer, having written for books including *Bloodwulf, Child's Play, ElfQuest, Justice League Quarterly,* and *Mad Dog.* He is the author of *Star Wars: The Essential Guide to Characters,* and writes frequently for many different magazines on science fiction and comics-related issues. Since 1991, he has also been the editor of *Gay Comics,* the largest gay-themed comic book.

Getting to where he is now wasn't easy for Andy, who grew up in a small community. "I knew about myself from a very early age," he says. "I didn't have a clear conception of what gay meant in terms of the community, but I knew that I was attracted to men. In Montana, where I lived, there just was no gay community. Growing up no one ever talked about it simply because it didn't seem to exist where we were. Of course, years later I found out that some of my high school friends were also gay, but then I just didn't think there were other gay people that I knew. I didn't learn about the gay community until I was an adult."

Retreating into the world of comic books as a way of dealing with his feelings of being different, Andy found in their pages other people who were outsiders in different ways. "*The X-Men* was about a group of people who were different," he remembers. "Each of the characters had some kind of special power that made him or her different from everybody else. People were afraid of them. People hated them. People had rallies against them. I could relate to that idea of being different and of being an outsider."

Still, he never saw gay people depicted in the comics he read. "There was nothing available to me as a young person who wasn't in a big city. The closest gay group was over two hundred miles away, and I couldn't get to it. There was nothing gay in my world for me to see and identify with, and that included the characters in my comic book world and in the science fiction that I read. Comic books had taught me all about other kinds of people—black people, Asian people, etc. Comics taught me a lot about what the world was like beyond where I lived. But they did not teach me anything having to do with my being gay. Later, when I got to know the writer of The *X-Men*, he talked about how he had meant that to be an allegory about all kinds of prejudice. I pointed out that there had been a black person on the team, an American Indian, an Asian, a blind person, a handicapped person. But there had never been a gay person. It would have really helped if there had been a gay member of the team."

Andy took art classes in high school and found that he had a talent for drawing. When he went to college at the age of sixteen, he majored in graphic design. He also took writing classes, which he enjoyed. He was soon drawing and writing his own stories, which became increasingly gay-themed and started to mirror his own feelings. "In college I was writing some comic series of my own. I had one character, a very masculine guy, who went from being sexually ambiguous to being bisexual to being gay. Then there was another character, who was essentially me, who went from being heterosexual to being sexually ambiguous, which is as far out as I felt comfortable being."

His feelings toward other men frightened Andy. "I was brought up Mormon and had a very strong religious background," he says.

"I didn't really think consciously about being gay. But I was drawing these supermasculine figures and having increasingly erotic fantasies about men. Eventually I came to a point where I thought, I'm either going to do this and go to hell, or I'm not going to do it and kill myself within the next couple months because I can't continue to live like this."

Andy decided to come out. "I felt I had to do it," he says. "I couldn't live any longer in fear that someone would discover the *Playgirl* magazines under my bed or pick up the well-thumbed-through issues of *The X-Men* and have them fall open to the pictures of Wolverine with his shirt off. I was completely terrified that somebody would find out about me and it would be all over and I would have no control over it. I decided that I wanted to be in control of it. All through my life, because I had been an outcast in so many ways, I did everything I could to control my own life. Everyone else was trying to take control over me, and I took back control over everything in my life until this one issue, my sexuality, was the last thing I wasn't in control of. I knew that I was either going to throw out the religious beliefs I had that said being gay was wrong or I was going to respond negatively by committing suicide. I chose to respond in a positive way, and as a result I am a much happier person. The things that I have accomplished in my life, both personally and professionally, would never have happened if I hadn't come out."

After making his decision, coming out happened very quickly for Andy. "I decided on April 15, 1988, that I was going to do something about my life," he remembers. "I wrote six letters responding to ads I found in a newspaper to meet other gay men. Two days later I met someone and talked to him. I quickly became involved in a gay discussion group that met on campus, which was funny because I had always known that a gay group met there and had always avoided even going near it out of fear that someone would see me there and know I was queer. Once I made the decision to come out, all of that terror I felt was gone. I was free of it all because I was in control."

Andy came out to the comic industry as well. He had been writing articles about the comic world for some time and decided it was time for the industry to address gay issues. "I came out in the comic industry in an article I wrote called 'Gay Characters and Gay Creators' for a magazine called *Amazing Heroes*," he remembers. "In the article, I traced the limited history of gay characters in comic books, and I interviewed some people who were gay in the industry. None of them would come out. At the end of the article, I quietly came out. That became a very big deal in the comic industry. That summer, at the largest annual comic convention in the world, the San Diego Comic Convention, I did the first ever panel on gays in comics, and it was their best-attended panel that year. Since then I've done the panel every year, and each year more and more people come out, including all of the people quoted anonymously in that original article."

Coming out professionally provided Andy with the opportunity to start featuring gay characters and storylines in the comics he wrote, something he promised himself he would do so that other young people would have the opportunities he never had to see gay people in their books. "The comic industry is an incredibly hard one to break into," he says. "I did get into it, and one of the things I promised myself was that, as often as I could, I would work in gay characters or gay storylines or even a simple positive gay joke. And I've been able to do that. For example, I was writing a comic book based on the movie *Child's Play*. In one of the books, I wrote in a scene where a police officer involved in the plot is shown at home with his lover and gives him a kiss on the cheek. It was a brief scene, but it was a big deal. I had to get all kinds of permission from the movie company and the movie's writer and other people. They went ahead with it, and there was no negative response to it from the readers. I did a *Quantum Leap* story in which the main character, Sam, inhabits the body of a lesbian the week of the Stonewall Riots. It was, and still remains, the most gay-positive comic book that has ever been published by a mainstream comic book publisher. I even

wrote an editorial for the inside front and back cover about the history of the gay rights movement and what the Stonewall Riots meant. That was a great thing to do."

Andy is proud of the fact that he has been able to feature gay subjects in his work. "A lot of the things I've done I've gotten really positive mail about. People have told me I help make a difference or that it's nice to know that there's somebody out there who cares. People write and tell me that I've shown them that there are gay people in comics or even other gay people out there at all, and that's wonderful. There has also been negative response, but overall I think that by coming out in the industry in a bold manner and never ever apologizing for who or what I am, I set myself up and out there as someone who had better be respected. I am not ashamed of being gay or of my talent as a writer, and if people want to hire me as a great writer, they have to take me as a gay man too."

Andy's advice to other gay people worrying about their sexuality is to have faith in yourself and to be honest. "Generally, your fears are going to be much greater than the realities. Not always, but usually. If you can learn to be independent enough to hide yourself from people, you can learn to be independent enough to show yourself to people." The rewards of being open about being gay, he says, are much better than the pain of being closeted. "If you learn to be proud of who you are, then you will eventually find people who respect that in you. It may not be right away, and it may put some speed bumps in your road, but you will eventually find people who don't care what you do in your private life; people only care that you are a good writer, or a good construction worker, or a good artist, or whatever you want to be. If people can learn to have the strength to stand up for who they are, then who they are will become their strength. If you aren't hiding anything, then there's nothing anyone can use against you. You are then operating from a source of strength and you can survive; you can triumph."

RELIGION AND SPIRITUALITY

Religion is a controversial topic. People have very strong opinions about their chosen faiths, and about the faiths of others, even when they usually know very little about other people's faiths. Even when people don't actively participate in their religion, they tend to have strong beliefs about what they think their religion is. More often than not, bringing up the subject results in arguments and hurt feelings on all sides.

This is particularly true when you bring up the subject of religion and the gay community. Many people in the gay community see religion in all of its forms as one of the biggest enemies we have. After all, religious leaders of many different kinds tell us that we are horrible sinners because of what we are. They say they don't want us in their churches, temples, or synagogues. Many of us grow up being told that homosexuals are evil, bad people who corrupt children, bring about the downfall of society, and quite rightly end up going to hell for what they are.

Because of these attitudes, there is a lot of resentment, anger, and hostility toward religion in the gay community. Many women and men feel hurt and outcast by religion and react by completely turning away from it. Others take out their frustrations by protesting against religious teachings. Some groups have even interrupted church services as ways of protesting the church's attitudes toward and treatment of gay people.

It's sad that so many people have been left out of religion. Our faith, or what we chose to believe in, can be one of the strongest and most wonderful parts of our lives. A strong faith, no matter what it is in, can provide us with comfort, strength, and a sense of well-being. Having this experience soured by hatred, bigotry, and fear is a very hurtful thing. But it doesn't mean we don't have a right to our spirituality.

At heart, most religions are concerned with teaching how to live positive, healthy lives, in which we learn to love ourselves, love others, and worship whatever higher power is involved for allowing us the ability to do these things. What do these teachings say specifically about homosexuality? That often depends on who is telling you what *they* think the teachings say. The teachings of Jesus Christ, for example, were first written down two thousand years ago in languages few people fully understand now. Over the years, these teachings were translated by many different people. Each person who translated them brought in his own interpretation or choice of words when deciding how to phrase the teachings. This has led to some changes in meaning as well.

For example, some people firmly believe that certain verses in the Bible say that homosexuality is wrong. Others say that isn't the case, and that these verses have been misinterpreted. Did Jesus really say that gay people are bad? People will argue that he did. They'll even show you Bible verses to prove it. But these verses are all just their interpretations of what Jesus or his followers said. Still, some people will always say that gay people are sinners and that we have no place in real churches.

Many things have changed about religion over the years, often because those things inconvenienced the people who claim to be leaders in those religions. For example, many religions used to forbid divorce or would not allow divorced people to be members of the religion. Then, when divorce started to become more common, and churches realized they wouldn't have many members or even leaders left if they kept out divorced people, suddenly all kinds of new rules were invented so that divorce wasn't such a big deal anymore. The churches admitted that maybe they were wrong about what they thought was true. The same holds true for religions with strict practices about what kind of foods people can eat, what they can and can't do, and what they have to believe. As more and more members of religions resist certain rules, they tend to fall away.

Sometimes these changes are good ones. For example, many religions now allow women to participate equally in religious activities, where even a few years ago only men were allowed to do so. We are now seeing more women becoming Episcopal priests, Jewish rabbis, and ministers in other faiths. This change happened because many women spoke up and demanded to be treated fairly. They demanded to be able to participate in their own faiths equally. But it took many years of bitter fighting for women to make other people admit that they deserved these rights, and there are still a lot of people who don't think women belong in these positions, including the Catholic Church.

Homosexuality is the last thing most churches have to scream about and point fingers at. For the most part they've given up on divorce, single mothers, and sex before marriage. And they're even starting to give a little about gays. Recently, after a gay rights group in England began publishing the names of gay priests, the Church of England (similar to the Episcopal

Church) announced that it was altering its policy toward the acceptance of gay and lesbian people and of gay clergy. They didn't say they had been wrong before; they just announced that gay people were acceptable to the Church of England. And many churches in the United States have slowly begun to relax their policies about lesbian and gay people.

So how do we develop healthy, productive religious lives if all we ever hear is that we don't belong in religion? For many years the general attitude among gay people was that we just had to leave religion forever. But today, many gay people have chosen to "take back" religion by forming their own groups that are based on traditional methods of worship. For example, there are now very active groups of lesbian and gay Catholics, Episcopalians, Jews, and even pagans. There is also an active gay church called the Metropolitan Community Church, with churches in many cities. These women and men find traditional ways of worshiping very fulfilling and meaningful, and they firmly believe that there is a place for them in those religions, despite anything other members of these groups might say about homosexuals.

These people do not accept the notion that God does not accept them the way they are. They understand that God loves everyone, and that it's people making up rules about what you can and cannot be in order to be a spiritual person who are at fault. Rather than fight to be included in their religions, they have chosen to form their own churches that are based in those religions but have their own special characteristics, ceremonies, and celebrations. Some of these groups are reluctantly recognized by their religions; others are not. But whether they are or aren't doesn't really matter. The women and men who have formed them and who find strength and joy in them don't need the approval of a pope or an archbishop or anyone else. They have the approval of the spiritual power they have chosen to worship.

Your spirituality is yours alone. You may share the same beliefs as others, but how you approach those beliefs is something you will develop over many years. You don't have to follow anyone else's set of rules. And never let anyone tell you that you don't have the right to worship as you want to. If you want to use a Jewish ritual to express your beliefs, then use that ritual and make it yours. If you want to use a Wiccan ritual, then use it. Don't ever let anyone tell you that you cannot participate in something because you don't belong. Your faith is between you and whatever higher power you choose to accept.

As gay people, we may never be fully accepted by mainstream religion. And while you don't have to worship anything or belong to any religion, you should know that you can if you want to. Never let anyone tell you that you don't belong, or that because you're gay or because you're lesbian you don't have a right to a fulfilling spiritual life. Don't reject all religion because some ignorant people try to tell you what God thinks. You can be gay and be Catholic. You can be lesbian and be Buddhist. You can be whatever you want to be, and you don't have to feel bad about it. It may mean disagreeing with what you've been taught and getting angry when people say hateful things about gay people. It may mean accepting that certain things about your religion are not what you believe, but continue to worship despite those things.

When it comes down to it, religion isn't about rules and regulations or about ceremonies and rituals. It's about feeling connected to something or someone larger than yourself. It's about getting something personal out of prayer, meditation, or other forms of worship. And no one can ever take that away from you, no matter how hard he or she tries.

The following books discuss many different aspects of religion and spirituality as it relates to the lives of gay and lesbian people.

BALKA, CHRISTIE AND ANDY ROSE, *Twice Blessed: On Being Lesbian or Gay and Jewish* (Boston: Beacon Press, 1989).

BOULDREY, BRIAN, ed., *Wrestling with the Angel: Faith and Religion in the Lives of Gay Men* (New York: Riverhead, 1995).

CHERRY, KITTREDGE AND ZALMON SHERWOOD, eds., *Equal Rites: Lesbian and Gay Worship, Ceremonies, and Celebrations* (Louisville, KY: Westminster John Knox Press, 1995).

DEAN, AMY, *Proud to Be: Daily Meditations for Lesbians and Gay Men* (New York: Bantam, 1994).

HELMINIAK, DANIEL A., PH.D., *What the Bible* Really *Says About Homosexuality* (San Francisco, CA: Alamo Square Press, 1994).

MCNEILL, JOHN J., *The Church and the Homosexual* (Boston: Beacon, 1993).

MCNEILL, JOHN J. *Freedom, Glorious Freedom: The Spiritual Journey to the Fullness of Life for Gays, Lesbians, and Everybody Else* (Boston: Beacon Press, 1995).

THOMSON, MARK. *Gay Soul: Finding the Heart of Gay Spirit and Nature* (San Francisco, CA: HarperSanFrancisco, 1995).

LIVING IN A STRAIGHT WORLD

No matter how many gay people we know or how many live around us, the fact is that we live in a world that is made up mainly of straight people. Yes, it's possible to spend your life almost entirely within the gay community. But we all still have to live in a world that is governed by straight society.

Why does this matter? It matters because it affects a lot of different things in our lives. Straight politicians decide what rights we should have. Straight people write articles about us and comment on our lives. Most advertisements, television shows, and movies are created for straight people. Most laws, such as marriage and adoption laws, are written with straight people in mind. We are constantly reminded that most of the world is straight, and sometimes it's easy to think that as gay people we just don't matter.

It also seems that if gay people take a step forward, they are pushed back two steps. We celebrate when a show like *Roseanne* features a lesbian kiss, only to hear that several sponsors have decided to pull their advertising from another show attempting to feature a similar storyline, causing the show to rethink having gay characters. We campaign for a presidential candidate like Bill Clinton because he promises to end the ban on gays in the military, only to have him back down and settle for a compromise. We applaud performers like Melissa Etheridge for coming out and showing that gay people can succeed, then have members of Congress vote not to allow government funding for art with gay content.

Gay people have made huge strides in society, and we make more every single day. But we have to keep pushing and fighting to hold onto what we have already fought for so hard. We've learned that we can't assume things will always be OK for us as gay people, and we know that there are people who want us to fail.

One way to deal with living in a straight world is never to leave the gay community. It is possible to live almost entirely surrounded by other gay people, doing gay things and ignoring outside problems or issues that don't affect our immediate lives as gay people. It's possible to block out everything except being gay.

Other people argue that when it comes down to it, we're just like straight people, and we should learn to live alongside everyone else without trying to have a separate community. There's at least some truth in this. Essentially, we are just like straight people in that we want to be able to live where we want to live, have the jobs we want to have, have families if we choose to, and generally be able to live our lives in the ways that make us happy people. And many gay people do live peacefully alongside their straight neighbors.

Unfortunately, there are just as many gay people who aren't able to live as they want to. Yes, we have come a long way as a community. But we still have people who want to see us pushed back into the closet. We still have people who want to pass laws making us invisible and making it acceptable to discriminate against us. We still have people who hate us.

Most of us have to live in both the gay and straight worlds, dealing with both straight and gay people and their various concerns and issues. Sometimes this can make us feel pulled in many different directions. Our straight friends might not understand our particular concerns. Our straight employers might not be as gay-positive as we would like. Our neighborhoods might not have as many gay people as we'd like them to.

Balancing our gay identities with the realities of living in a straight world can be hard. So how do we do it? We form a network of other gay people. We find friends who are also gay, and we make connections with other members of the gay community. No one says you have to talk only to gay people or deal only with gay people. But it can make a big difference in your life if some of the people around you are also gay.

For example, there are some issues that you might have trouble discussing with your doctor if she isn't gay. Finding a gay doctor not only makes you feel more comfortable about taking care of your health, it makes you a part of the gay community. Similarly, you might feel more comfortable taking your car to a gay mechanic, eating in gay-owned restaurants, living in a predominantly gay neighborhood, or shopping at gay-owned stores. I like living in a neighborhood with other gay people because it reminds me that I am not alone. I like going to my dentist, who is gay, and I switched doctors from a straight one to a gay one when my old doctor made negative comments about gay people. Now I know I have someone who really cares about my health and any health issues I might have as a gay man.

All of these things make me feel that I belong to the gay community. I feel connected to other gay people, and I feel that a lot of the people in my daily life share something important with me. On a larger scale, what this does is make our community closer. By helping and supporting one another, we are creating a stronger community. And when our community is stronger, we are better able to stand up for our rights, and we are more united as a family.

Not everyone in our lives has to be gay, nor should they be. We should have all kinds of people in our lives. And not all of us live in places where we can have gay dentists and lawyers and grocers. But some of you will want to live within the gay community, and you should know that it is possible to do that if you want to. You will still be living within straight society, but you will have the benefit of being surrounded by other gay people who can support you.

If you find yourself living somewhere where you feel completely cut off from other gay people and gay society, the thing to do is try and remain connected through things like books, music, films, and magazines. By reminding yourself of all that being gay can mean, you are creating an identity that will help you live a happier life.

As gay people, we have many opportunities to make a difference in our own lives and in the lives of others. We can become involved in our local communities, creating stronger ties to other gay people and working to make life easier for gay people around us. We have opportunities for expressing our ideas and thoughts and celebrating what being gay means. We also have the opportunity to show the larger world that gay people are an important part of every community, and that gay women and men deserve to be as respected as anyone else. We can speak up for what we believe and for what we want; we can elect public figures who understand our needs, and we can make our voices heard.

Living in a predominantly straight world doesn't mean we have to be silent and put up with things that bother us or with people who pretend we don't matter. It doesn't mean that we have to take a backseat to other people just because there are more of them than there are of us. It doesn't mean we have to feel isolated and outnumbered and overwhelmed. It just means we have to form our own communities. It means we have to keep ourselves informed about issues that concern us. It means we have to make our own circles of friends who make us feel good about being gay and who remind us that being gay is a wonderful, positive thing.

SAN FRANCISCO, CA — Thomas Roche

In San Francisco, lesbian and gay culture is woven so deeply into the life of the city that it is often hard to separate it out from the rest of city life. The gay community has a very strong voice in city life and politics, and gay issues are taken seriously by politicians and law-makers. Being out in San Francisco may be easier than almost anywhere in the country, and San Francisco has for years been seen as *the* place to live as a gay man or woman because of its relaxed atmosphere for gay people. Even in the most conservative middle-class neighborhoods, gay or lesbian couples often walk down the street holding hands. Certain neighborhoods carry diversity much further, at times taking on the feeling of a libertine utopia for gay people. To be sure, homophobia and even violence still exist in San Francisco; but for the most part, the city feels, to many, more accepting of sexual diversity than almost anywhere else in the country.

The casual nature of San Francisco's lesbian, gay, bisexual, and trans-gendered communities makes it easy to be out, but it doesn't always make it so easy to decide how to get involved. As in any big city, there are so many choices that it can be hard to decide where to begin. And despite the size of the community, it often seems as if everyone knows everyone else, which can contribute to feeling like an outsider if you're the new kid in town. The best way to meet friends and join the community is to open yourself to new experiences and conversations wherever you are, rather than expecting one bar, club, or interest group to provide you with everything. Joining a service organization as a volunteer may also provide you with a chance to meet people while helping the community.

San Francisco's gay community likes to celebrate, and the city boasts a huge and extremely diverse Gay Pride Parade in June. Groups march under a variety of banners of ethnic, political, and social affiliations, and the Women's Motorcycle Contingent—"Dykes on Bikes"—never fails to make a stunning impression, with their bikes firing up like the sound of morning thunder. Other annual events, like the Castro Street Fair and the Folsom Street Fair, serve as celebrations in summer and fall.

So where do you start your search for San Francisco's gay community? The gay/lesbian/bisexual/transgendered (GLBT) communities in San Francisco have as their epicenters the neighborhoods known as "the Mission" and "the Castro." While Castro Street is a legendary fixture in San Francisco gay life, it is actually part of an array of neighborhoods that stretches from the neighborhoods of Duboce Park to Bernal Heights, south of Market Street to Twin Peaks. While the Castro is a mixed neighborhood with many businesses for all sexual minorities, women-owned and lesbian-oriented businesses tend to be in the Mission, a larger and more ethnically, socially, and economically mixed neighborhood east of the Castro.

South of Market harbors most of the leather and S-M-oriented businesses and clubs in San Francisco, as well as most of the dance clubs and mixed nightclubs. Polk Street is another center of gay male life, though things can be a bit rougher on Polk than in other areas because of the transient characters in the street.

The best way to get involved with the community is to visit some of the GLBT businesses in town. They will almost invariably have a bulletin board with listings of events, readings, meetings, movies, performances, and the like, for a variety of groups. While it's always difficult to meet people in social or performance situations, it's much easier when those attending are of a reasonably focused group or all share a common interest. By attending some events, you're sure to meet people who can introduce you to other things the community has to offer.

Another method for finding out what's happening in San Francisco's gay community is to read the local gay papers—the *Sentinel* and the *Bay Area Reporter*, both of which are free and easy to find in stores, clubs, and restaurants around town. The *San Francisco Bay Guardian* and the *SF Weekly*, the other two big free papers in town, have huge numbers of ads and listings of educational and recreational events. Other handouts and newsletters come and go (the most notable being *Oddyssey*). Another good source of information is the magazine *Q San Francisco*, which along with listings contains articles about queer life in the city.

You can also find listings of organizations and events at popular queer stores like Good Vibrations or Modern Times, both on Valencia; A Different Light bookstore on Castro; and any number of cafés in the Mission, especially on Valencia Street. Many gay businesses allow people to post notices about upcoming events, and many businesses hold their own events, including lectures, discussion groups, book and poetry readings, and workshops. Just stopping into a bookstore or having a cup of tea at a café can bring you into contact with many different aspects of the gay community.

San Francisco's gay community is a very friendly and active one, and there are many groups devoted to helping people come out and become involved in gay life. Examples of some specific resources that might help you get involved with the community include the following:

> 18th Street Services on Church Street serves as a counseling and resource center for the gay community.

> San Francisco Sex Information (415-989-7374) is a nonprofit educational and informational phone line, which operates Monday through Friday 3:00 P.M. to 9:00 P.M. A highly trained staff will answer your questions on a variety of issues ranging from orientation to sex practices, and provides referrals to a wide range of Bay Area organizations or professionals. SFSI also offers excellent training for those who wish to be phone volunteers. In a fifty-two-hour training course, you learn about sexual issues, and you have the opportunity to meet people of stunningly diverse backgrounds and orientations.

> The Gay/Lesbian/Bisexual/Transgendered Switchboard at the Pacific Center for Human Growth (510-841-6224) also offers referrals and provides basic information about some events.

> Lavender Youth Recreation and Information Center (LYRIC) (415-703-6150) is a lesbian, gay, bisexual, transgendered, and questioning youth organization.

Their phone line provides helpful recorded information on a variety of issues. LYRIC also operates a Queer Youth talkline at (415) 863-3636, Tuesday 4:00 P.M. to 9:00 P.M. and Monday though Saturday 6:30 P.M. to 9:00 P.M. The talkline provides an opportunity for Bay Area young people to talk to other young people about sexual orientation and identity issues.

> San Francisco boasts a highly active bisexual community, and the Bay Area Bisexual Network and Bisexual Political Action Group (BABN) (415-703-7977) is a good place to start finding it. They also publish a great political/sex 'zine called *Anything That Moves*.

> For transgendered resources, try the Educational TV Channel (510-549-2665), a social and educational support group for all transgendered persons and cross-dressers. They offer classes and social events centered around transsexual and transgendered issues.

> San Francisco also has a wide array of political groups for the GLBT community: the Lesbian Avengers, GLAAD, ACT-UP, and many other groups have very active branches here. Gays and lesbians are very actively involved in every level of politics in the city, from local school boards to the mayor's office, and there are all kinds of opportunities for becoming involved in gay politics. There are many other resources and opportunities that can be found in the papers or on fliers at local businesses.

As in any city, once you start to find it, the gay community in San Francisco will come to you. The most casual trip down Castro Street can provide you with a dozen ideas of where to go and what to see in order to become more involved. Something as simple as seeing a movie at the Castro Theater can make you feel, even in a small way, like part of the community, and that can give you the confidence you need to get involved.

THOMAS S. ROCHE has been involved in the San Francisco Bay Area S-M/gay community for five years. He has served as a phone volunteer and lecturer for San Francisco Sex Information, performs regularly at readings and benefits, and writes for such local magazines as Black Sheets *and* Slippery When Wet.

ENDINGS

We live in a world where it isn't always easy to be gay. There are people who want us to think that there's something wrong with us. There are people who don't want us to have equal rights. There are people who want to tell us the "right" way to live. It takes a lot of courage and self-respect to be gay or lesbian, and sometimes it's really hard. I think most gay people probably have days when we think, if only for a second, that being straight would be a whole lot easier. But I doubt many of us would take the chance to become straight if it were offered.

Being gay can bring many special things to your life, things you would never have as a straight person. The gay community is filled with wonderful people doing exciting things with their lives, and you can be a part of that. As a gay person, you have qualities and experiences that are totally different from the ones straight people have. Yes, in many ways we are just like everyone else. But in many ways we are uniquely different. Uniquely special. Uniquely gay.

If you are in a situation right now where you feel all alone or depressed, I hope that you see that you aren't really alone. You may have to wait a little while before you meet other gay people, but that day will come. Sometimes it seems as if it will take forever, but it won't. There will be a day when you can be who you are and explore who you are. No matter where you live or who you are, you are part of a community that stretches all around the world, a community made up of many different kinds of people. And no matter what anyone tells you, you are special and you are worth caring about.

Perhaps you are already exploring who you are as a lesbian or gay person. If that's the case, then I applaud your courage and hope that you are having a wonderful time learning about yourself and about what being gay means. For you I hope this book has been a reminder that being gay has its ups and downs, just like anything else, and that the bad days are made up for by the days or even single moments when we can really enjoy who we are. I hope it has reminded you of all the wonderful possibilities for your life, and maybe even given you some new ideas or inspirations.

If you are just beginning to explore what being part of the gay community means, I hope that this book has given you some ideas of how to begin, of things to do, and of the possibilities waiting for you. I hope that you will use it as your guide and return to it from time to time.

Whoever you are, I hope that you are well and happy.

FOR FURTHER EXPLORATION
MAGAZINES

The following magazines represent a sample of the many different periodicals available of interest to lesbian and gay people. Some of these magazines, including *The Advocate* and *Out,* are often available at public libraries. Many are found in newsstands, and all are available by writing to the addresses provided and asking for subscription information.

The Advocate (6922 Hollywood Boulevard, 10th Floor, Los Angeles, CA 90028). *A biweekly newsmagazine featuring the latest news of interest to gays and lesbians, as well as articles, interviews, and reviews. The foremost gay newsmagazine in the world.*

Amethyst: A Journal for Lesbians and Gay Men (191 Howard Street NE, Atlanta, GA 30317). *Features articles, fiction, poetry, photography, and essays relating to the gay experience.*

Art & Understanding: The International Magazine of Literature and Art about AIDS (25 Monroe Street, Albany, NY 12210). *Features essays, articles, interviews, photography, and reviews of art and literature related to or inspired by the AIDS crisis.*

Christopher Street (PO Box 1475, Church Street Station, New York, NY 10008). *Features essays, articles, and fiction by and about gay men.*

Curve (2336 Market Street, Suite 15, San Francisco, CA 94114). *A glossy, life-style magazine featuring articles, essays, interviews, and news of interest to lesbians.*

50/50 (2336 Market Street, #20, San Francisco, CA 94114). *Features articles, reviews, essays, and interviews on subjects of interest to lesbians, gay men, and bisexuals.*

Fountain: An Alternative Source for Women (2221 Wilton Drive, Fort Lauderdale, FL 33305). *Not just for lesbians; this magazine has strong lesbian content and includes articles on a variety of subjects ranging from women's health to political issues affecting women of all kinds.*

Genre (PO Box 18449, Anaheim, CA 92817-8449). *For gay men, this slick magazine features articles, interviews, entertainment reviews, and short fiction.*

Girlfriends (3415 Cesar Chavez, Suite 101, San Francisco, CA 94110). *A progressive magazine for lesbians featuring articles, interviews, and essays about sex, politics, health, and entertainment.*

HUES (Hear Us Emerging Sisters) (PO Box 7778, Ann Arbor, MI 48107-8226). *Not exclusively lesbian; this magazine for women of color features articles on subjects ranging from dating to fashion, political issues to lesbian young people.*

Lambda Book Review (1625 Connecticut Avenue NW, Washington, D.C. 20009). *A review of lesbian and gay books and issues of interest to gay writers, readers, publishers, and booksellers.*

Men's Style (PO Box 993, Edison, NJ 08818-0993). *A life-style magazine for gay men, featuring articles on fashion, entertainment, and health and numerous photo spreads.*

Out (110 Greene Street, Suite 600, New York, NY 10012). *A gay version of* Vanity Fair, *this magazine for both lesbians and gay men features articles, interviews, and essays about many different topics, ranging from politics to fashion, entertainment to sports.*

Poz (PO Box 1279, Old Chelsea Station, New York, NY 10113-1279). *A magazine written by and for people living with HIV/AIDS. Features articles, essays, and interviews about HIV/AIDS-related topics.*

Tapestry Journal: For All Persons Interested in Cross-dressing and Transsexualism (PO Box 229, Waltham, MA 02154-0229). *The primary magazine for the transsexual/transgendered community, this entertaining and informative magazine contains articles of interest to transsexual and transgendered people and features profiles of transsexual and transgendered people. Focuses primarily on men who dress or live as women.*

Transsexual News Telegraph (41 Sutton Street, #1124, San Francisco, CA 94104-4903). *A newspaper/newsletter dealing with the transsexual community.*

FOR FURTHER EXPLORATION
B O O K S

The following lists feature books that might be of interest to you. All of these books, as well as the books listed in the text, can be found in lesbian and gay bookstores or ordered from gay bookstores. Many of them can also be found in regular bookstores. You can also order these books, and many others like them, through the mail from the following gay bookstores:

A Different Light
151 West 19th Street
New York, NY 10011
(212) 989-4850

489 Castro Street
San Francisco, CA 90069
(415) 431-0891

8853 Santa Monica Boulevard
West Hollywood, CA 90069
(310) 854-6601

A Different Light provides free catalogs, and you can order most gay and lesbian titles from them by calling 800-343-4002 twenty-four hours a day. You can also order books from A Different Light via computer by reaching their World Wide Web site at http://www.adlbooks.com/~adl.

Lambda Rising
1625 Connecticut Avenue, NW
Washington, D.C. 20009

Lambda Rising has many out-of-print lesbian and gay titles, as well as all new titles. You can order books from them by calling 800-621-6969 or by checking out their online bookstore on America Online by selecting the keyword *gaybooks*.

COMING OUT
The following books deal with many different aspects of coming out.
Some are about how to come out. Others are personal accounts of
people who have come out or who have had family members come out.
Others are helpful for the friends and families of people who come out.

Dew, Robb Forman, *The Family Heart: A Memoir of When Our Son
Came Out* (New York: Ballantine, 1994).

Eichberg, Rob, Ph.D., *Coming Out: An Act of Love* (New York: Plume,
1990).

Fairchild, Betty and Nancy Hayward, *Now That You Know: What
Every Parent Should Know about Homosexuality* (San Diego, CA:
Harcourt Brace, 1989).

Griffin, Carolyn Welch, Marian J. Wirth and Arthur G. Wirth,
*Beyond Acceptance: Parents of Lesbians and Gays Talk about Their
Experiences,* (New York: St. Martin's Press, 1986).

MacPike, Loralee, *There's Something I've Been Meaning to Tell You*
(Tallahassee, FL: Naiad, 1985).

Penelope, Julia and Susan J. Wolfe, eds., *The Original Coming Out
Stories* (Freedom, CA: The Crossing Press, 1989).

Signorile, Michelangelo, *Outing Yourself: How to Come Out as
Lesbian or Gay to Your Family, Friends, and Coworkers* (New York:
Random House, 1995).

GAY AND LESBIAN YOUNG PEOPLE
The following books contain material about what it is like to grow up
lesbian or gay.

Bernstein, Robin and Seth Silberman, eds., *Generation Q: Inheriting
Stonewall* (Los Angeles: Alyson Publications, 1996).

Carlip, Hillary, *Girl Power: Young Women Speak Out* (New York: Warner
Books, 1995). Contains essays, poetry, fiction, and interviews with many
different kinds of young women, including lesbian and bisexual women.

Chandler, Kurt, *Passages of Pride: Lesbian and Gay Youth Come of Age* (New York: Times Books, 1995).

Cohen, Jaffe, Danny McWilliams and Bob Smith, *Growing Up Gay: From Left Out to Coming Out* (New York: Hyperion, 1995). A humorous look at growing up gay by the comedy team known as Funny Gay Males.

Due, Linnea, *Joining the Tribe: Growing Up Gay and Lesbian in the '90s* (New York: Anchor, 1995).

Heron, Ann, ed., *Two Teenagers in Twenty* (Boston: Alyson Publications, 1995).

Romesburg, Don, ed., *Young, Gay, and Proud* (Boston: Alyson Publications, 1995).

Singer, Bennett L., ed., *Growing Up Gay/ Growing Up Lesbian: A Literary Anthology* (New York: The New Press, 1994).

Sutton, Roger, *Hearing Us Out: Voices from the Gay and Lesbian Community* (Boston: Little, Brown, 1994).

AUTOBIOGRAPHY AND BIOGRAPHY
The following books are just some of the many wonderful biographies and autobiographies of lesbians and gay men available.

Allison, Dorothy, *Two or Three Things I Know for Sure* (New York: Dutton, 1995). Allison is the National Book Award-nominated author of the novel *Bastard Out of Carolina.*

Barrett, Martha, *Invisible Lives: The Truth about Millions of Women-Loving Women* (New York: William Morrow, 1990). A collection of profiles of lesbians from different walks of life.

Blue, Adrianne, *Martina: The Lives and Times of Martina Navratilova* (New York: Birch Lane Press, 1995). Navratilova is the most successful women's tennis player in the history of the game.

Boy George, *Take It Like a Man* (New York: HarperCollins, 1995). Boy George was the lead singer of the group Culture Club, and is now a successful solo performer.

Cammermeyer, Margarethe with Chris Fisher, *Serving in Silence* (New York: Penguin, 1994). Cammermeyer was one of the first women to challenge the military's ban on lesbians serving in the armed forces.

Cossey, Caroline, *My Story* (Boston: Faber & Faber, 1991). The auto-biography of the British model known as "Tula," a transgendered woman whose ongoing battle to win the right to marry in the United Kingdom has earned international attention.

Crisp, Quentin, *The Naked Civil Servant* (New York: New American Library, 1983). Crisp was an out gay man in London at a time when being gay was punishable by imprisonment. He is one of the gay community's first publicly out figures.

Fricke, Aaron, *Reflections of a Rock Lobster: A Story about Growing Up Gay* (Boston: Alyson Publications, 1981). The classic story of Fricke's com-ing out and the battle he waged to take a male date to his school's prom.

Jackson-Paris, Rod and Bob, *Straight from the Heart: A Love Story* (New York: Warner Books, 1994). Both successful weightlifters and professional bodybuilders, Rod and Bob Jackson-Paris share their personal stories.

Jones, Bill T. with Peggy Gillespie, *Last Night on Earth* (New York: Pantheon, 1995). Jones, an African American, is one of the most successful choreographers in the dance world.

Lorde, Audre, *Zami: A New Spelling of My Name* (Freedom, CA: The Crossing Press, 1983). Lorde, who died of breast cancer, was a wonderful poet and storyteller.

Louganis, Greg with Eric Marcus, *Breaking the Surface* (New York: Random House, 1994). Louganis won several Olympic gold medals for his diving, and is now a successful actor.

Leeming, David, James Baldwin: *A Biography* (New York: Henry Holt, 1994). Baldwin is one of the most popular African-American writers, and the author of the gay-themed novel *Giovanni's Room*.

Monette, Paul, *Becoming a Man: Half a Life Story* (San Diego: Harcourt Brace Jovanovich, 1992). Monette, who died from AIDS, won the National Book Award for this eloquent account of his life as a gay man.

Preston, John, *Winter's Light: Reflections of a Yankee Queer* (Hanover, NH: University Press of New England, 1995). Preston, who died from AIDS, tells the story of his life as a gay man in New England.

Reid, John, *The Best Little Boy in the World* (New York: Ballantine, 1986). The classic book about one man's coming out as gay.

Schumacher, Michael, *Dharma Lion: A Biography of Allen Ginsburg* (New York: St. Martin's Press, 1992). A fascinating look at the life of the celebrated poet.

Souhami, Diana, *Gertrude and Alice* (New York: HarperCollins, 1991). Stein and Toklas were lovers, and this biography recounts their amazing relationship and their lives in Paris surrounded by some of the world's most famous and infamous writers, actors, and artists.

Steffan, Joseph, *Honor Bound: A Gay Naval Midshipman Fights to Serve His Country* (New York: Villard, 1991). Steffan was thrown out of the Navy after revealing his homosexuality.

White, Edmund, *The Burning Library: Essays by Edmund White* (New York: Vintage, 1995). Some of the best essays by one of the gay community's most respected writers.

REFERENCE

The following books provide information on a wide variety of topics that may be of interest to lesbian and gay readers.

The Alyson Almanac: *The Fact Book of the Lesbian and Gay Community* (Los Angeles: Alyson Publications, 1996).

The Editors of Out Magazine, *The Gay and Lesbian Address Book: Make Contact with Over 3500 Leaders in the Arts, Business, Politics, Activism, Culture, and Much More* (New York: Perigree, 1995).

Blumenfield, Warren J. and Diane Raymond, *Looking at Gay and Lesbian Life* (Boston: Beacon Press, 1993).

Curry, Hayden, Denis Clifford and Robin Leonard, *A Legal Guide for Lesbian and Gay Couples* (Berkeley, CA: Nolo, 1995).

Dotson, Edisol, ed., *Putting Out: The Essential Publishing Resource for Lesbian and Gay Writers* (Pittsburgh: Cleis Press, 1994).

Faderman, Lillian, ed., *Chloe Plus Olivia: An Anthology of Lesbian Literature from the Seventeenth Century to the Present* (New York: Viking, 1994).

Fahy, Una. *How to Make the World a Better Place for Gays and Lesbians* (New York: Warner Books, 1995).

Green, Francis, ed., *Gayellow Pages* (New York: Renaissance House, 1995). Contains addresses and phone numbers for many different kinds of gay and lesbian organizations, hotlines, etc. across the United States and Canada.

Grega, Will, *Gay Music Guide* (New York: Pop Front, 1995). *A listing of all kinds of music by lesbian and gay performers or of interest to gay listeners. Includes addresses for ordering by mail.*

Marcus, Eric, *Is It a Choice? Answers to 300 of the Most Frequently Asked Questions about Gays and Lesbians* (New York: HarperCollins, 1993).

Mickens, Ed, *The 100 Best Companies for Gay Men and Lesbians* (New York: Pocket Books, 1994).

Murray, Raymond, *Images in the Dark: An Encyclopedia of Gay and Lesbian Film and Video* (Philadelphia, PA: TLA, 1994).

Preston, John, *The Big Gay Book: A Gay Man's Survival Guide for the 90s* (New York: Plume, 1991).

Sherrill, Jan-Mitchell and Craig A. Hardesty, *The Gay, Lesbian, and Bisexual Students' Guide to Colleges, Universities, and Graduate Schools* (New York: New York University Press, 1995).

Stewart, Steve, *Gay Hollywood Film & Video Guide* (Laurel Hills, CA: Companion, 1994).

Summers, Claude J., *The Gay and Lesbian Literary Heritage* (New York: Henry Holt, 1995).

Witt, Lynn, Shirley Thomas and Eric Marcus, *Out in All Directions: The Almanac of Gay and Lesbian America* (New York: Warner Books, 1995).

RESOURCES

This section contains information on some national organizations that provide information and services to lesbian, gay, bisexual, and transgendered people. Because addresses and phone numbers change, and because new organizations are created so often, it is a good idea to check that an organization you are interested in is still in operation. It is also a good idea to check with your local gay and lesbian community center, if you have one, to see if any new organizations are available in your area. If you find that a group or hotline is no longer in service, contact another organization and find out what else is available in your area.

If you do not have a local gay and lesbian community center, and cannot find any listings for gay organizations in your area, a good organization to contact is *Parents, Families, and Friends of Lesbians and Gays (P-FLAG),* 1101 14th Street NW, Suite 1030, Washington, DC 20005. They can also be reached by phone at (202) 638-4200 or by e-mail at pflagntl@aol.com. P-FLAG operates more than 300 groups around the country offering support to lesbian and gay people and their families, and they can help you locate other useful groups in your area.

You might also want to check out *Gayellow Pages,* a directory of many different resources available to gay people. It can be found in most gay bookstores or ordered from Renaissance House, Box 533 Village Station, New York, NY 10014 or by calling (212) 674-0120.

If you are a young person looking for more information, you might want to get a copy of *You Are Not Alone: National Lesbian, Gay, and Bisexual Youth Organization Directory.* The directory is published by *The Hetrick-Martin Institute* in New York City, and can be ordered by calling (212) 674-2400 or writing to The Hetrick-Martin Institute, 2 Astor Place, New York, NY 10003. The Hetrick-Martin Institute is devoted to serving gay, lesbian, bisexual, and transgendered young people, and may be able to provide information on groups for young people in your area.

Some active national groups serving the gay community are listed below. By contacting these groups, you may be able to find out about any related or affiliated local groups in your area.

American Civil Liberties Union-Lesbian and Gay Rights Project
132 West 43rd Street, New York, NY 10036
(212) 944-9800

The ACLU works for many causes, including the rights of gays and lesbians. If you are involved in a legal case involving gay rights, or have a question regarding gay people and the law, the ACLU can help. There may be a local ACLU office in your area, or you can call the head-quarters in New York for more information.

The American Educational Gender Information Services, Inc. (AEGIS)
PO Box 33724
Decatur, GA 3033-0724
(404) 939-0244

Founded in 1990, AEGIS is a nonprofit organization dedicated to serving the needs of all transgendered and transsexual persons, as well as to helping professionals involved in the areas of transgendered work. The group publishes booklets on transgendered/transsexual issues, and publishes the magazine *Chrysalis*. Among other things, they maintain a database of information of interest to the transgendered community, and operate the National Transgender Library & Archive.

American Indian Gays and Lesbians
PO Box 10229, Minneapolis, MN 55458-3229

Asian/Pacific Lesbians and Gays, Inc.
Box 433, Suite 109, 7985 Santa Monica Boulevard
West Hollywood, CA 90046-5111

Digital Queers
584 Castro Street, Suite 150, San Francisco, CA 94114

Digital Queers is a national group of gay, lesbian, bisexual, and trans-gendered computer professionals and technology aficionados.

Gay and Lesbian Alliance Against Defamation (GLAAD)
150 West 26th Street, Suite 503, New York, NY 10001
(212) 807-1700

GLAAD monitors and combats incidents of homophobia in movies and on television.

Gay and Lesbian Arabic Society
Box 4971, Washington D.C. 20008

Human Rights Campaign (HRC)
1012 14th Street NW, Washington, D.C. 20005
(202) 628-4160

A national political organization for gay men and lesbians. The HRC focuses on issues such as AIDS, civil rights, and anti-gay activity.

The International Foundation for Gender Education (IFGE)
PO Box 229, Waltham, MA 02154-0229
(617) 894-8340 or (617) 899-2212
E-mail to ifge@std.world.com

Founded in 1978, IFGE is an educational and charitable organization addressing crossdressing and transgender issues. They publish materials relevant to transvestite and transgender issues, including *Transgender Magazine*, and sponsor the annual Coming Together convention. Further, they operate an international information and referral clearing-house, and speakers bureau, and offer emergency peer counseling and ongoing volunteer opportunities.

National Coalition for Black Lesbians and Gays
Box 19248, Washington, D.C. 20036

National Coming Out Day
PO Box 8349, Santa Fe, NM 87504

National Coming Out Day is October 11. This organization can give you information on any local events taking place.

National Gay and Lesbian Task Force (NGLTF)
1734 14th Street NW
Washington, D.C. 20009-4309
(202) 332-6483

NGLTF works to secure equal rights for gay men and lesbians. Their
focuses include reducing anti-gay violence, supporting lesbian and gay
families, ensuring privacy and civil rights, and ending the military ban
on gay people.

National Latino/Latina Lesbian and Gay Organization
PO Box 44483, Washington, D.C. 20026
(202) 544-0092
North American Multicultural Bisexual Network
584 Castro Street, Box 441, San Francisco, CA 94114-2558

Rainbow Alliance of the Deaf
PO Box 14182, Washington, D.C. 20044-4182

Trikone: Gay and Lesbian South Asians
PO Box 21354, San Jose, CA 95151
(408) 270-8776